THE CENTER IS EVERYWHERE

CELTIC SPIRITUALITY FOR THE POSTMODERN AGE

Bruce G. Epperly

THE CENTER IS EVERYWHERE

CELTIC SPIRITUALITY FOR THE POSTMODERN AGE

Bruce G. Epperly

Parson's Porch
Books
Cleveland, TN

Parson's Porch Books
121 Holly Trail, NW
Cleveland, TN 37311

ISBN: Softcover   978-1-936912-08-7

This book was printed in the United States of America.

To order additional copies of this book, contact:

Parson's Porch Books
1-423-475-7308
www.parsonsporch.com

CONTENTS

AN INVITATION TO ADVENTURE

You are about to embark on a uniquely postmodern adventure. Postmodern spirituality is profoundly experiential, fluid, dialogical, and relational. Uncomfortable with fixed doctrines and institutional orthodoxy, the postmodern spirit seeks holiness and wholeness in experiencing God in ordinary as well as dramatic experiences, mediated through daily tasks, intimate relationships, clusters of friends gathered in times of celebration and pain, and moments of awe and wonder in which new energies and insights stream into our lives.

Postmodern spirituality experiences the Divine in moments of creative transformation in which prayer, worship, contemplation, service, and healing embrace, in an ever-moving now, both ancient wisdom and future hope, in ways that engage all the senses as portals of revelation. Faith is fluid, emerging, and evolving, as personal and communal spirituality integrates the wisdom of Christianity with that of Buddhism, Islam, Judaism, Hinduism, new spiritual movements, contemporary physics, complementary medicine, and earth-based faiths.

At such a time as ours, an emerging, vital, transformed and transforming Celtic spirituality provides a way of wholeness for pilgrims within and beyond Christianity.

The way of Celtic Christian spirituality finds divine revelation in the cells of bodies, the glistening waters, the colors of the rainbow, and the human imagination. Celtic Christianity experiences God in all things and all things in God. God is found in the rising of the sun and the rising of the Crucified One.

I invite to join me in a pilgrimage of the spirit that embraces the wisdom of Celtic spirituality in dialogue with the emerging wisdom of process-relational theology, contemporary physics, global and complementary healing, and religious pluralism. Inspired by postmodern, process-relational spirituality, this Celtic spiritual pilgrimage joins theology and spirituality in dynamic, lived experience and personal narrative. Though well-grounded in constructive Christian theology, this text calls you to experience first-hand a lively spirituality that is both intimate and global through "prayers for the pilgrimage." Based on evolving and emerging Celtic wisdom, these prayers invite you to experience the spirituality of ancient Celtic pilgrims for this time and place. It is my hope that these prayers will inspire you to receive and claim your vocation to be a creative partner with an Adventurous God in healing the world.

The words that follow are the gift of a lifetime of spiritual experiences, inspired by numerous relationships over the years. Every word has arisen in the day to day dialogue with my partner in life and ministry of over thirty years, Kate Epperly. Kate is my companion, inspiration, and spiritual friend, for all the seasons of life. I have learned to love the every day life in its simplicity an evolving relationship with our son Matt, manifest in the journey from bedtime stories and little league baseball to philosophical hikes, golf matches, hospital rooms, and celebrations of love with his wife Ingrid and young son Jack. Much of this text arose in conversations with my spiritual friend, Anna Rollins, whose care for family and friendship and imaginative spirit has been an inspiration for nearly a decade.

I honor my mentors and teachers, and their love of wisdom and quest for a theology and spirituality for the postmodern world: John Cobb, David Griffin, Bernard Loomer, Marie Fox, Howard Thurman, and John Akers. I am grateful to colleagues, who I first met in the classroom, and whose work and friendship has been an inspiration for over thirty years: Jay McDaniel and Catherine Keller. I am grateful for the inspiration of J. Philip Newell, Esther de Waal, John Bell, and Alexander Carmichael, who have made the Celtic spirit come alive for me.

I am grateful for seven and one-half years at Lancaster Theological Seminary. During that time, my colleagues on the faculty at Lancaster Theological Seminary, especially President Riess Potterveld, Dean Edwin David Aponte, David Mellott and Kathy Harvey Nelson supported and encouraged creativity and innovation in my professional adventure. I appreciate the everyday support of my administrative assistant, April Bupp, whose practical wisdom enabled me to venture forth in the "adventures of ideas."

Many of these of these insights were explored in the emerging progressive Christian congregation where I served as co-pastor from 2004-2010, Disciples United Community Church in Lancaster, Pennsylvania. Through it all, the love and support of spiritual friends has enabled me to live out a postmodern Celtic vision

Bruce Epperly
Advent 2010

CHAPTER ONE

PILGRIMS OF THE SPIRIT

A pilgrim prepares to embark for an unknown land. She is filled with both anticipation and apprehension as she begins her journey. There are wonders and surprises on the adventure that awaits her, but there are also rumors of strange beasts and demons along the path she will take. As she leaves her familiar home, she pauses a moment to listen to the Divine Spirit that guides and protects her. She then invokes the presence of the Encompassing God. With her right index finger she draws a circle around herself as she turns to the right, dancing in the circle of the sun's rising. She chants an ancient prayer to the God whose motherly love and fatherly care will guide and protect her every step on the journey ahead:

> The encompassing of God and God's right hand
> Be upon my form and my frame;
> The encompassing of the High Ruler and
> the grace of the Trinity
> Be upon me abiding ever eternally.
> May the encompassing of the Three shield me in my means,
> The encompassing of the Three shield me this day,
> The encompassing of the Three shield me this night
> From hate, from harm, from act, from ill,
> From hate, from harm, from act, from ill.[1]

---

[1] Adapted from Esther de Waal, *The Celtic Vision*, (Liquori, Missouri: Liquori Publications, 2001), p. 109.

Though she may fear the darkness of the night and the strange shadows of the woods, she knows that her journey will be encompassed by the Divine Pilgrim, the Lively Encircling God, for whom even the darkness is light.

Threatened with death by a local chieftain, another pilgrim of the spirit invokes the Encompassing God. Though he trusts his soul to God, this pilgrim's daily path is fraught with dangers that tempt him to lose heart. With every footstep, he takes courage from his own affirmation of faith:

> Christ behind and before me,
> Christ beneath and above me,
> Christ with me and in me,
> Christ around and about me,
> Christ on my left and on my right,
> Christ when I rise in the morning,
> Christ when I lie down at night,
> Christ in each heart that thinks of me,
> Christ in each mouth that speaks of me,
> Christ in each eye that sees me,
> Christ in each ear that hears me.[2]

Heartened by God's sustaining presence in his own life, this pilgrim, - known to us - as St. Patrick, envisages

---

[2] Robert Van de Weyer, *Celtic Fire* (London: Darton, Longman, and Todd, 1990), p.80.

God's love transforming and embracing even the hearts of his enemies. Encircled by God's protective love, Patrick knew that he was safe regardless of the unexpected and expected challenges and threats of everyday life.

Hundreds of years pass and another pilgrim prepares for a perilous journey. Though her travels seldom take her beyond her workplace, the shopping center, and the local schools, each day she confronts the challenges of self-discovery, learning new patterns of relationships, and experiencing daily healings for herself and her family. As she goes forth, uncertain of what awaits her, she draws a circle around herself and her loved ones each morning as a reminder that God will be their constant companion throughout the day. Within the circle of love, she knows that God will provide her with the resources to face every challenge. Even amid conflict and struggle, she knows that God's circle encompasses her in every moment of life.

Two thousand miles away from my home in Lancaster, Pennsylvania, I gaze at the mountains that encompass Ring Lake Ranch in Wyoming. As I sit upon the stone butte that was once a sacred place for Native American vision quests, I visualize a healing light surrounding myself, my wife Kate, my son Matt, and my closest friends.3 I reflect on the challenges we face as I imaginatively encircle each one in the divine love that enlightens and transforms. In the tradition of the Celtic

---

3 The first drafts of this text were written at Ring Lake Ranch, a spiritual retreat and conference center near Dubois, Wyoming, and about 100 miles from Yellowstone National Park. To learn more about this holy place, visit the website at www.ringlake.org.

11

practice of "caim," the encompassing or encircling prayer, I visualize each person within the Divine circle of grace, healing, and protection that has neither beginning nor end. Despite my concerns about the journeys each of my loved ones must take, I know deep down that the Divine Circle will surround and protect us each day of our holy adventure. In the spirit of the ancient Celts as well as those young adults who prayed for vision and vocation at this holy place, I open my heart to the Encircling One with a twenty-first century encircling prayer.

Encircling Companion, surround and guide my loved ones.
Let your circle protect them from all ill.
Let your wisdom guide their thoughts and actions.
Let your love heal and transform them.
Guide their pilgrimage one step at a time.
Let them see your presence in every event
And be your healing presence to all they meet.
May they always know that their home is with you
And that your home is within them
In this life and beyond.

An ancient wisdom giver once affirmed that "God is a circle whose center is everywhere and whose circumference is nowhere." While the precise origin of this spiritual affirmation is unknown, it addresses the universal spiritual quest that joins both safety and adventure. Some scholars suggest that this affirmation originated with the ancient Greeks, while others attribute it to Christian spiritual guides such as Athanasius, Augustine, Iranaeus, Meister Eckhardt, Votaire, Pascal, and Nicholas of Cusa.

But, like most spiritual truths, this affirmation reflects the universal wisdom that embraces a plurality of religious and philosophical traditions.

I ask you to reflect on these inspiring words for a moment as you ponder God's love encircling and guiding your own life. Let them awaken your spirit, calm your mind, and open your heart to your own Deepest Center. Take a moment to breathe as you ponder their meaning for your life today.

> God is a circle
> Whose center is everywhere
> And whose circumference is nowhere.

Take a moment to repeat those words, allowing their wisdom once again to permeate your body, mind, and spirit. Let them become companions on your own spiritual pilgrimage today and in the future.

> God is a circle
> Whose center is everywhere
> And whose circumference is nowhere.

LIVING IN THE DIVINE CIRCLE

The image of the circle reminds us of eternity and wholeness. We glimpse it in the Celtic cross and in the Native American spiral pictographs at Ring Lake Ranch and throughout Western North America. We are inspired by its mystery as we walk the sacred labyrinth. Within the

Divine Circle, we are safely embraced. The storms may howl and enemies threaten, but within the circle, we have a sanctuary and a home. Known or unknown, God is at the center – of our lives, our daily pilgrimages, and the unknown future that stretches before us.

Sioux visionary Black Elk, whose own spiritual journey embraced the wisdom of both Christianity and the Native American heritage, describes the importance of the Divine Encircling to those young persons who made vision quests at throughout the Americas.

> Everything an Indian does is in a circle, and that is because the Power of the World always works in circles, and everything tries to be round. Everything the Power of the World does is done in circles. The sky is round, and I have heard that the earth is round like a ball, and so are all stars. The wind, in its greatest power, whirls. Birds make their nests in circles, for theirs is the same religion as ours. The sun comes forth and goes down again in a circle. The moon does the same, both are round. Even the seasons form a great circle in their changing. The life of man is a circle from childhood to childhood and so it is in everything where power is.[4]

---

[4] John Niehardt, *Black Elk Speaks* (Lincoln: University of Nebraska Press, 1961), pp. 198-199.

The Sacred Circle encompassed young Native American and Celtic adventurers on their perilous vision quests and still enfolds the dying on as they take their first steps on their journey beyond the grave. The Holy Circle brought justice and safety to the tribe, community, and nation. God's Sacred Circle still encompasses spiritual pilgrims, like the Celtic *peregrines,* who set forth on wild adventures, according to Philip Newell, in search of their place of resurrection.[5]

The times of our lives and the seasons of the earth are circular as well as linear in nature. Living from the center, we find that all life is holy and vibrant, and that Divine guidance inspires us in each moment. Centered in God, the Celtic pilgrim Brendan voyaged on unknown seas, trusting that God would be his partner on a holy adventure. Wherever his skiff landed, Brendan and his companions knew that the Holy One who had guided their course would be waiting for them when they disembarked on new lands.

In that spirit, African American mystic Howard Thurman, counseled his anxious and impatient students simply to "simmer." To the sagely Thurman, simmering meant waiting quietly for signs of the passionate and faithful presence of God. For Thurman, simmering was centering, quietly resting in God's presence and awaiting God's wisdom. In the warmth of God's presence, light and heat are one and we discover our own true spiritual

---

[5] J. Philip Newell, *The Book of Creation: An Introduction to Celtic Spirituality* (New York: Paulist Press, 1999), 29.

compass. In simmering and centering, we find our path. In silence, vitality emerges. Divine Love awakens us to adventure and surprise. In Divine centering, all things find their home, even amid the most perilous journeys.

LIVING FROM THE CENTER

But, how difficult it has become for twenty-first century persons to find their sacred center! Just think of your own life and the lives of your closest friends and family members. Our spiritual geography mirrors our physical mobility. We seldom sit still or stay in one place for very long. We move from coast to coast, changing jobs, friends, marriages, and life partners. We are overwhelmed by too many possibilities for entertainment on cable television, Facebook, our iPod and blackberry, the internet, and the media. But, as we surf from channel to channel or scroll from one app to another, nothing truly satisfies us. Even when we stay in one place, we are still on the move, contemplating the next encounter, relationship, achievement, position, show, or social event. But, within all our busy-ness, we long for something more! We yearn for something solid and inspiring around which to center our lives.

Although I am by nature a contemplative, I still occasionally catch myself multi-tasking with abandon. As I sit in my living room recliner, bathed in the morning sun, I sip coffee, check the latest news and weather on TV, access messages on my cell phone, read my e-mail and Facebook updates, and listen to see if my wife Kate has awakened. Despite its great benefits, the information age has become a source of fear and fragmentation for many persons today. We check cable news programs hourly, anxious about terrorist attacks or the slightest change in the weather or stock market. Such instant knowledge provides little comfort and is no substitute for the wisdom of the ages. Advances in communications technology glut us with information overload, but give us few resources to respond to the crises of the day. We witness the wondrous diversity of experience, nationally and globally, but lack a stable center around which to organize this data. More than ever, we need a circle within which to find our home and a center to give us peace and wisdom. Within this sacred circle, dislocation and disorientation are embraced and become the materials for empathy and creative transformation.

Biblical scholar Walter Brueggemann notes that the dynamic wisdom of the Psalms involves the dynamic interplay of orientation, disorientation, and new orientation.6 His words remind us that we are not the first persons to seek a spiritual center in tumultuous times. Humankind has always sought a Divine circle to give us the security and courage we need to face life's greatest challenges and embark upon life's greatest adventures.

Twenty five hundred years ago, the author of Psalm 46 sought a spiritual center in the midst of his own chaotic world. As his familiar world disappeared, the Psalmist

---

6 Walter Brueggeman, *Praying the Psalms* (Winona, MN: St. Mary's Press, 1993).

discovered the Faithful Center who would be his companion in sorrow and celebration.

> God is our refuge and strength,
> A very present help in trouble.
> Therefore we will not fear, though the earth should change,
> Though the mountains shake in the heart of the sea;
> Though its waters roar and foam,
> Though the mountains tremble with its tumult.
> There is a river whose streams make glad the city of God,
> The holy habitation of the Most High.
> God is in the midst of the city;
> It shall not be moved;
> God will help it when the morning dawns.
> The nations are in an uproar, the kingdoms totter;
> God utters the divine voice, the earth melts.
> The Lord of hosts is with us;
> The God of Jacob is our refuge....
> "Be still and know that I am God!
> I am exalted among the nations,
> I am exalted in the earth."
> The Lord of hosts is with us;
> The God of Jacob is our refuge.

What comes to mind when you read these words? I reflect on a phone call I received early in the morning of September 11, 2001. My son, studying at Georgetown University in Washington D.C. just ten miles from our home at the time in Potomac, Maryland, roused me from my morning writing with the words, "Turn on the television. A plane just crashed into one of the towers of the World Trade Center." My first response was to assure him it that was simply a random plane crash that would not threaten our own lives. A few minutes later, I was shocked to see a second plane strike the World Trade Center in "real time." Suddenly, a third plane struck the Pentagon just a few miles away in Northern Virginia and a fourth plane was rumored to be on the way to attack the White House or Capitol. The earth shook, the oceans foamed, and the nations were in an uproar. The universe shrunk to dimensions of the television news reports as I anxiously pondered when and where the next attack would come.

Over and over that day and many days since 9/11, our information technology has given citizens of Canada and the United States more "real time" crisis information than we can process creatively. We are continually pulled off center, numbed, and disassociated by reports of weapons of mass destruction and terrorist schemes as well as natural disasters such as tsunamis, earthquakes, and mudslides. It seems that there is little we can do to respond creatively, even if we are able to hold our spiritual and emotional center. We do what we can to respond by working for peace and justice and stocking up on canned goods and water. But, still we fear what the future will bring – the color coded terrorist alerts and the reports of deaths in Southeast Asia, Haiti, and Darfur remind us of the vulnerability of all that we cherish.

Six years after the September 11 attacks, I receive another phone call, this time from Ingrid, our son Matt's new wife of just three months, telling me that x-rays have found a large, likely cancerous mass in his chest. My world is once again rocked to the core. My hands tremble and my heart races as I call my wife Kate, who is overseas on a spiritual pilgrimage with Celtic theologian Philip Newell

on the Isle of Iona. As I packed for the two hour drive to
Washington D.C., I felt like those Celtic pilgrims who set
sail on the high seas without a rudder to guide them.
Although the path was uncharted and uncertain as I entered
the frightening world of cancer, I sought God's center and
guidance so that I could support my son and his wife and be
a faithful partner to Kate.

Our faith in God's presence reminds us that
somehow amid the storms of personal and planetary life, we
can discover a center that holds and a circle that
encompasses all that we fear. Courage, compassion,
commitment, and love can still prevail over the feelings of
death, fear, and disassociation arising from the negative
information glut. "God is in the midst of the city; it shall
not be moved. God will help it when the morning dawns."

A Gentle and Presence was at work, bringing
persons back to their center even as the planes struck their
targets, buildings collapsed, and air travel was plunged into
chaos . That same presence led relief agencies and ordinary
citizens to aid victims of tsunamis and earthquakes. The
Holy Companion inspired fire fighters, police officers,
chaplains, and office workers to risk their lives in New
York. Ordinary people from all walks of life were inspired
to gather for prayer vigils and perform acts of kindness and
comfort for strangers in New York, Sri Lanka, Myanmar,
Haiti, and Thailand. In the aftermath of terrorist attacks,
God's circle of love invited persons in the United States to
challenge racism by reaching out to their Muslim neighbors
in care and protection. In the midst of radical
disorientation, whether political, economic, or personal, the

voice of a new orientation emerges. "Be still and know that I am God."

The Encircling Presence of God reminds us that we are safe, strong, and loved, within the circle of God's encompassing care. As I sped to the Washington D.C. hospital in the early hours of the morning, I breathed deeply, inhaling God's peace and wisdom, praying for strength and guidance to share God's encompassing love with my son and his wife. In my imagination, I visualized a circle surrounding Matt and Ingrid as well as Kate who would be flying from Glasgow, Scotland, to Washington D.C. In that circle, I knew that, despite my fear, I would find wisdom and courage for the days ahead.

In the wake of the attacks of September 11th, spiritual guide Jean Shinoda Bolen, invoked the Holy Center which endures even the greatest calamity.

> At this time of mourning
> May we be connected to each other,
> May we know the range and depth of feelings
> in ourselves and in each other.
> For there is vulnerability, fear, love, rage, hatred,
> compassion, courage, despair and hope
> In ourselves, in each other, in the world.
> May we know our most authentic feelings
> And voice them when we speak.
> May we tap into soul and spirit
> When we are silent together.
> May healing begin in us.
> May we form and become a center.
> Begin by holding hands in a circle
> (even two people can be one),
> Be silent and feel the clasp and connection

Of hands and heart.
Then each in turn
Speak for yourself
And listen to each other.
Put judgment aside.
Remember that anything voiced
That you may want to silence
May be a silenced part of yourself.
Sing what spontaneously wants to be sung.
And end each circle as it was begun.
Hold hands once again, hold silence
(for meditation, contemplation, prayer).
Invite blessings.
Until we meet again.[7]

Whether during moments such as those following 9/11, the Southeast Asian tsunami, the Haitian earthquake, or in the wake of a personal tragedy such as a diagnosis of cancer or unexpected job loss, many of us discover anew that "God is a circle whose center is everywhere and whose circumference is nowhere." As we inscribe a circle of quiet strength around us, we find our own personal center, and experience once again the Divine Love that permeates our lives and joins every center in love. "God is our refuge and strength, a very present help in trouble. Therefore we will not fear," for God's center is everywhere! As I entered the hospital to see my son, praying for courage and calm, I visualized once again God's encircling companionship as I prayed, "I inscribe a circle around me and claim God's

---

[7] Jean Shinoda Bolen, "Circle Invocation," *The San Francisco Jung Institute Library Journal* 20:3 (2001), p. 4.

center within me and manifest it with every breath." As I walked down the hallways to my son's hospital room, I visualized a circle of Divine Love surrounding him and Ingrid as I prayed, "God surround them with your everlasting circle of love and protection." I found peace as I steered into the storm.

TRUSTING THE HOLY ADVENTURE

During these days of chaos and transformation, the spiritual vision of Celtic Christianity and its encompassing God inspires and guides our personal and planetary journeys. Like many persons today, the ancient Celts were wanderers of body, mind, and spirit. The name "keltoi," from which the word "celt" emerges, means "stranger," and long before the time of Jesus, these ancients wandered upon strange lands in search of spiritual homelands.

With the coming of Christianity, many of these Celtic travelers claimed the name, "peregrine," pilgrim, to describe their spiritual adventures as followers of ever-wandering and encompassing Christ. Wanderers of the spirit set sail in small, rudderless boats from Ireland and Scotland without compass or map, trusting the Holy Adventure to breathe upon the waters and through the winds to guide their crafts safely to their true spiritual homes. Trusting the wisdom of the Wind, they discovered, as feminist spiritual guide Nelle Morton proclaims, that "the journey is home." Journeying by land and sea, they sought their "place of resurrection," their personal place of spiritual rebirth, the one "thin place" where eternity spoke their true names, and revealed the infinite circle of living and dying, and rising again within the adventure of each new day.

Trusting the wisdom that breathes through all things, the Celtic spiritual guides found divine inspiration and protection even in the most unexpected situations. Profoundly iconoclastic, they believed that the Holy Adventure burst through the boundaries of ritual, authority, and established belief system.8   They affirmed that the God who lured them into wildernesses of land and sea breaks through every human convention with the promise that there is always something more to discover in ourselves, our companions, and in the Divine Adventure itself. Poets and pilgrims of the Unbounded Spirit, these Celtic adventurers were as free as the wind that propelled their journeys. They saw themselves as companions of the Cosmic Christ, who charted humankind's path into the Divine Mystery. Their polestar was the liberating Spirit-breath of God.

> The wind blows where it chooses, and you hear the sound of it, but you do not know where it comes from or where it goes. So it is with everyone who is born of the Spirit. (John 3:8)

Authentic spirituality frees our spirits to love,

---

8 I use the term "Holy Adventure'" as one word for the Living God. For more on the Holy Adventure, see Bruce Epperly, *Holy Adventure: Forty-one Days of Audacious Living* (Nashville: Upper Room, 2008).

appreciate, and care. It pushes us beyond the lifeless past to the ever-living future of God's frontier. Today, the ancient Celts, as well as the spiritual wanderers of primeval America, guide us on a journey that is both personal and planetary.

CELTIC WISDOM FOR A POSTMODERN TIME

The story is told of European travelers who hired African tribesman to be their porters on a safari through wilderness lands. After a number of long marches, the Europeans were astonished when the porters decided to rest for the day. Ruled by clocks and schedules, they could not understand the reticence of their native employees until the chief porter revealed "we have traveled so quickly in so little time that we need to let our souls catch up with our bodies."

Today, we need to let our souls catch up with the radical intellectual, cultural, technological, political, and personal changes of our times. Though we may swirl about in perpetual white water, we can still find a quiet center from which to navigate life's changes. We can trust the ancient wisdom of the Celts even as we embrace the insights of contemporary physicists and progressive, process-relational spiritual guides. The emerging spiritual wisdom of our time portrays the universe as a community of communities. Relationship and interdependence are fundamental to the nature of things. Every part contains the imprint of the whole. Each thought and action radiates across the universe, shaping the future of ourselves and God's own Holy Adventure. There are no small adventures in a relational universe. The flapping of a butterfly in my Lancaster yard creates a pattern from which sunshine or showers may emerge not only in Amish country but in the Grand Tetons and Canadian Rockies. Consciously or not, we find comfort and healing from the gentle currents of grace that rise from the prayers and good wishes of friends far and near.

From this perspective, God is no longer envisaged as somewhere "out there" far from human joy and misery, but everywhere and in all things, giving birth in each moment to the universe. Each being is *a* center of the universe, revealing the divine in its creativity, liveliness, and interdependence. Even shattered moments and tragedies reveal an urge toward healing and beauty. The wisdom of Celtic spirituality is echoed in contemporary spiritual approaches that suggest that this lure toward wholeness is the origin and destiny of each creature and of the cosmos as a whole. There is a still point in each moment's flux and flow which is divine, deep, good, and whole. The insights of progressive Christians, process-relational theologians, and physicists echo the spirit of ancient Celtic Christians and invite us to a become participants in a creative synthesis of ancient wisdom and twenty-first century cosmology and theological reflection.

As I write these words today, I remember gazing from the rough--hewn desk in my cabin at Ring Lake toward the shimmering waters of Trail Lake and snow--capped peak of Middle Mountain in the distance, filled with the radical amazement at awesome beauty of Life in its Wholeness. On an August night at Ring Lake Ranch, I roused myself to witness a meteor shower. With the Celtic pilgrims, Native American visionaries, and contemporary cosmologists, I was overcome with the vastness of the universe. In that moment, I caught a glimpse of the deeper realities of myself and the universe - God-breathed, spirit-filled, and enchanted just like the stars. The heavens declare the glory of God and each moment reveals timeless wisdom. I am a cell in the dynamic spirit-filled body of God, utterly finite and ephemeral. Yet, my ephemeral self is infinite in heritage and destiny as I live out my unique role as a pilgrim in the Cosmic Adventure.

TRUST YOUR HORSE

The morning after the meteor shower, my sense of the call to adventure became personal and concrete. At Ring Lake Ranch, mornings are filled with hiking, horseback riding, and prayer. As the group was invited to join in morning ride, my wife Kate nudged me and said, "now is the time." In my nearly fifty years of life, I had only been on a horse once, and that was for the duration of five minutes. I had planned to focus on writing, rather than riding, during my stay as seminar leader at the ranch. I didn't even plan to go near the horses! But, adventure – in the echo of my wife's voice - called me forward to new possibilities. I was a bit apprehensive as I walked toward the corrals. After all, it is easier to write about intellectual adventures than actually participate in a real flesh and blood adventure! I had to visit the outhouse – "Taj Ma Hole"-

twice before I mounted my horse! But, for the next two hours, I was led on an adventure one step at a time over gentle paths and steep hills. As I mounted my horse, the wranglers reminded me to "trust your horse," and I did even as I held on for dear life! I repeated my riding mantra "trust your horse, trust your horse, trust your horse" each step of the rocky path. I trusted my horse and he proved faithful and sure. But, trusting "Jake" was just a small part of my quest to trust the universe and claim the reality of God's Adventure whenever I feel nervous. I also needed to trust my own inner wisdom and strength. Although this was a small adventure in scheme of things, for this desk-bound theologian the ride was nevertheless an important adventure in companionship with the same Spirit that guided Celtic skiffs and wandering pilgrim feet.

Psychologist Erik Erikson stated that the most important foundation for creativity and adventure is the experience of basic trust. Original trust, like the original goodness of the universe, is a virtue that encompasses all things. Our trust in others is stunted if we fail to see our own inner beauty and competence. Trust in ourselves falters if we believe that the universe is deaf to our cries and unconcerned with our well being. We cannot fully trust the universe as a whole if the part of the universe that we experience in ourselves and in our environment lacks a fabric of wholeness and strength amid change and insecurity. We find courage and strength when we discover that we live in circles of love, trust, and adventure, grounded in the Center that is everywhere.

In the pages ahead, the ancient words "God is a circle

whose center is everywhere and whose circumference is nowhere" will become the spiritual affirmation for your personal and cosmic adventures. As you reflect on this ancient wisdom, I hope you will discover that you are always at the Divine center where God's wisdom is your deepest reality. As you explore new horizons and follow surprising paths, I pray that you will find that God's care and protection is your constant companion. If you journey with God's Center, you will find that whether you look across the universe, the dinner table, or a hospital bed, you will experience the face of God because the ever-present Center is the deepest reality within every creature and everything you see.

I invite you to journey with me on a cosmic pilgrimage, guided by the Holy Adventurer who lives, moves, and has its being in all things. With ancient, contemporary, and future pilgrims of the spirit, we begin by drawing a circle of love, blessing, and protection around us, as we affirm:

> I on thy path, O God.
> Thou God in my steps.
> Bless me, O God
> The earth beneath my foot,
> Bless me, O god,
> The path whereon I go.[9]

---

[9] Esther de Waal, *Every Earthly Blessing,* (Harrisburg, PA: Moorehouse, 1999), p. 9.

PRAYERS FOR PILGRIMS

Ancient wisdom comes alive for those whose seek the Eternal and Ever-changing Adventure. At the conclusion of each chapter, you will be invited to participate in prayers, meditations, and blessings that arise from the partnership of Celtic spirituality, postmodern inspiration, and process-relational spirituality. In these prayers, you will find a lively spiritual foundation for the insights of today's postmodern, mission-oriented, and emerging Christianity. Indeed, these various meditative prayers are an attempt to forge authentic postmodern Christian spiritual practices. In the freedom of God's unbounded spirit, let your experience breathe freely through each exercise so that each prayer or visualization exercise reveals the Holy Adventure personally to you and, then, through your life to others. Your own Center is strong, wise and able beyond your imagination, and in God the circumference of your adventure is nowhere.

Exercise One -Drawing a circle of blessing. The traditional Celtic "caim" or encircling prayer involves simply drawing a circle around yourself or another person physically or in your imagination. This encircling prayer is grounded in your awareness of the constant companionship and protection of the Holy Adventure.

Take a moment to draw a holy circle around yourself or, imaginatively, around a loved one, as I did for Matt during his hospital stay. You may use a traditional or contemporary prayer of encircling, such as the one with which this book begins. You may also choose to write and read your own personal prayer for yourself or another. But, in any case, the power of a spiritual tradition often finds its most lively expression when we embody it from our deepest spirit and in the language of our own hearts. Whatever you do, please invoke the words from the depths of your heart and let them radiate through and beyond you in outward sound as you dance in the Divine Circle.

One traditional prayer of encompassing invokes our awareness of the Ever-present Companion with these words:

> The God of the Elements' guarding,
> The loving Christ's guarding,
> The Holy Spirit's guarding,
> Be cherishing me, be aiding me.[10]

A contemporary prayer of encompassing proclaims the loving nearness of God in every situation:

> Circle of love,
> Open my heart.
> Circle of wisdom,
> Enlighten my mind.
> Circle of trust,
> Protect my path.
> Circle of healing,
> Grant me new life.

An important element in the spiritual journey is our blessing of others. To bless another is simply to place them

---

[10] Esther de Waal, *Celtic Vision,* p. 104.

in our hearts with the intention that they be surrounded, enlightened, and inspired in body, mind, and spirit by the Encompassing Love of God. I often say the following prayer as I visualize friends and family embraced by the Divine Circle. I symbolically encircle them in my imagination by imaging myself drawing a circle around them using flowing dance-like movements.

Circle of love
Encompass _____.
May your love well up within her/him
May your passion enlighten her/him.

Circle of healing
Encompass _____.
May your healing touch rest upon her/him.

Circle of protection
Encompass _____.
Surround _____ with your eternal safety
Protect her/him from all temptations and ills
Give her/him courage and strength
To live always from Your safe and powerful center.

A Circle of Light. When a friend or family member is in physical, emotional, spiritual, or relational crisis, I surround her or him with a radiant circle of Divine light. I envisage this light encompassing, permeating, strengthening, and protecting them. I affirm on their behalf the Divine Light that enlightens every creature and overcomes every fear and threat.

Exercise Two -Centering in the Circle. Every faith tradition has repetitive chants, affirmations, and prayers.

In invoking these words over and over, their deepest truth is grounded in our daily experience. Beginning with conscious repetition, these words eventually become an unconscious melody that shapes our perception of ourselves and reality. In order to ground the vision of this book, I invite you to take time throughout the next week to repeat the words:

> God is a circle
> Whose center is everywhere
> And whose circumference is nowhere.

Let these words become your constant companion. If you find yourself anxious or afraid during the week ahead, draw a divine circle around yourself, either in your mind's eye or by moving your hands around yourself to inscribe a circle in space, as you remember these words. Let them be a healing talisman for your journey. If you are feeling anxious about a loved one or world situation, visualize a circle surrounding that person or situation as a way of affirming and supporting God's healing presence.

Exercise Three - Small Adventures. In truth, there are no small adventures. Every adventure of spirit and geography begins with a dream and a few small steps. When God is our companion, we can do anything; but still the Divine Adventure begins right where you are. What seems a small adventure to others– such as riding a horse or speaking up at a meeting– may seem like a perilous journey for you. But, the Great Adventure begins with the smallest of steps or, perhaps, simply a "yes"when the stranger on the seashore asks,"Will you follow me?"

Take time to be still and place yourself in the Divine Quiet from which all things flow. Safe in this circle of quiet, reflect upon your life gracefully and lovingly. Visualize a life adventure that you have previously undertaken – going away to college, sharing your heart with another, challenging an injustice, mountain climbing, horseback riding, healing a relationship, standing up for your truth. Remember your feelings and the internal and external challenges that you experienced when you embarked upon this adventure. But, also remember the joy of that adventure!

Now, visualize your current life situation. It too is part of a Holy Adventure. Ponder the question: What adventure is Life calling you toward? Do not judge this adventure in terms of size or challenge, or what others have achieved. Though it may not be the greatest adventure that currently lies before you, it is an important adventure, and it is connected with every other adventure on the horizon. What are your feelings about undertaking this adventure? What internal and external challenges lie before you? What are your greatest fears?

In the quiet circle, imagine yourself and the adventure you are undertaking surrounded by God's circle of protection and love. God's Holy Adventure will encircle you wherever you go. Visualize yourself moving within the circle and taking the first steps on this great adventure. Trust that you have the strength and guidance you need wherever you go.

You may also choose your own spiritual affirmation for the journey. It may be as simple as my "trust your horse" or "God is with me on this ride" or "God guides me in my job search." You may also use one of the encircling prayers found in this chapter. I often use traditional Native American prayer invoked by Black Elk.

God guides me on my job search
With visible breath I am walking.
In a sacred manner I am walking.
With visible tracks I am walking.
In a sacred manner I walk.[11]

Know that wherever the journey takes you and whatever challenges you face, God's Circle of love surrounds, protects, and empowers you. You are within God's circle, for "God is a circle whose center is everywhere and whose circumference is nowhere."

---

[11] John Niehardt, *Black Elk Speaks*, p. 4.

CHAPTER TWO

LIVING FROM GOD'S CENTER

Cosmic Stardust
Awesome Wonder
God Within Me
Love Is Now

These words, inscribed on a Celtic cross fashioned by artist Colette Brooks, express the deepest nature of things –of the clouds scudding across the sky, the eagle in flight, the face of your beloved, the cat sleeping on your lap, the cells of your own body. As revelations of the Light of the World, we are *cosmic stardust*, finite and temporary, perpetually perishing. But, we are also eternal reflections of God's 14 billion year Holy Adventure. The whole universe conspires to create each moment of our lives. We were there in the beginning, as divine possibility and children of the cosmic birth. The light of life that enlightens all things (John 1:9), God's creating and illuminating light, shines in and through us. As Celtic theologian and spiritual guide Philip Newell asserts, "At the heart of all that has life is the light of God. It dapples through all of creation."[12]

We are *awesome wonder*. A sung prayer, I learned while studying at the Shalem Institute for Spiritual Formation in Washington D.C. simply affirms, "I thank you God for the wonder of my being."[13] Filled with the "radical amazement" that Rabbi Abraham Joshua Heschel believed was the heart of religious experience, I experience awesome wonder in my wife Kate, in my son Matt and grandson Jack, in my relationship with my closest spiritual friend, in the osprey flying across the horizon to feed its young, in the blue waters of the lake, and in the wind blowing through pine trees outside my cabin at Ring Lake. Each one of us is unique in the cosmos, charting an incredibly new and awesome journey from birth to eternity. As you look at your life and relationships, what inspires awesome wonder? Where does life amaze, astound, and inspire you? Where do you see yourself as awesome and beautiful?

God within me. Deep down, often hidden beneath our self-doubt and misdirected desires to be someone else, the Spirit is singing and bringing forth our lives moment by moment. As Nikos Katzanzakis says in *St. Francis*, "we come from God and go to God, and sing to help us find our

---

[12] J. Philip Newell, *The Book of Creation,* p. 3.

[13] For more information on the Shalem Institute for Spiritual Formation, contact www.Shalem.org. This chanted prayer was written by spiritual director and voice teacher Isabella Bates, who was for many years my wife Kate's spiritual director.

way." The Spirit constantly sings the melodies of love, creativity, and wonder in sighs too deep for words." (Romans 8:26) Each one of us is a theophany, a revelation of God, and an icon through which the Divine Spirit shines.

Love is now. The essence of our being is love. Life is the dynamic weaving together of unity and diversity, individuality and interdependence, and solitude and community. Love gives birth to galaxies, meteor showers, grizzly cubs, freckles, and human faces. In the rhythm of the one and the many, love parents forth holograms and universes each moment of the day. The Divine Love that brings forth the stars and planets is the primordial parent of each child. Each moment is a miracle, each child a singularity - all things deeply woven in the fabric of Divine Love.

THE HOLY HERE

And so it is that each one of us is called to use our imagination to claim the mystic vision: "God is a circle whose center is everywhere, and whose circumference is nowhere." God's center is *everywhere.* At their depths, all things are wonderful, cosmic, beloved, and divine. In the vastness of the cosmos, our particular center of experience often seems so insignificant. Yet, long before the discovery of holograms, black holes, and far off galaxies, Hebrew sages sought to hold together both the wonder of finite and mortal humankind with the incomprehensible immensity of the universe.

> O Lord, our Sovereign,
> How majestic is your name in all the earth!
> You have set your glory above the heavens,
> Out of the mouths of babes and infants
> You have founded a bulwark because of your foes,
> To silence the enemy and the avenger.
> When I look at the heavens, the work of your fingers,
> The moon and stars that you have established:
> What are human beings that you are mindful of them,
> Mortals that you care for them.
> You have made them a little lower than God,
> And crowned them with glory and honor.
> You have given them dominion over the works of your
>   hands.
> You have put all things under your feet,
> All sheep and oxen,
> And also the beasts of the field,
> The birds of the air and the fish of the sea,
> Whatever passes along the paths of the seas.
> O Lord, our Sovereign,
> How majestic is your name in all the earth!

Hurtling through the vastness of the universe, our little planet seems of no consequence. Humankind, who but a moment ago existed only as a possibility in the Divine Imagination, seems little more than a temporary visitor in the evolving planetary journey. So, who are we as individuals and as communities? Little more than a mote of dust in human history or a microorganism on the face of the earth, we arise and perish from generation to generation, on a mortal planet in an inconspicuous corner of the universe. But, is this the whole story of our lives and our planet?

Overwhelmed by the awesomeness of the universe and its Creator, the Hebraic sage also discovers the amazing wonder of each human life. You are cosmic stardust! You are a little lower than God! You are a moving image of eternity, a dynamic mirror of divine creativity! Amid the immensity of the universe and tragedies of daily life, we are not alone, for "God is a circle whose center is everywhere and whose circumference is nowhere." Your life is encircled and embraced in God's Everlasting Life and Love that treasures and preserves all that is good. You are at the center of God's Holy Adventure. What happens on this planet truly matters, despite our apparent cosmic insignificance.

Theologians use the term "omnipresence" to describe God's intimacy with all things. Yet, far from being an abstraction, the doctrine of divine omnipresence affirms that:

> God is everywhere.
> God is right where you are.
> God is within you.
> God is your deepest reality.
> God breathes through each thought and emotion.
> God inspires you each moment of the day, even when you are unaware of it.
> God is present in your life just as God was present in the life of Jesus.

Mystics have told us that all things reveal Divine wisdom. As the German mystic Meister Eckhardt proclaimed, "All things are words of God." Celtic spiritual guides affirmed that each person is a "thin place" where time and eternity give birth to ever-changing beauty. Each person is a miracle, uniting divine creativity and the cosmic journey. This is surely the deep personal meaning of the "image of God" in humankind. Some speak of God enshrined in the heavens, untouched by life's imperfections. Others name God the "wholly other," beyond time and place, and the imagination, with no point of contact between divinity and humanity. Still others in the modern world exile God to the irrelevance of a Saturday's father who dazzles the children on good days with miracles and wonders and terrifies them the next day with plague and pestilence. Dramatic in "his" occasional manifestations, this absentee parent abandons us for extended periods, observing our personal and planetary journeys from a distance until arbitrarily deciding to perform a miracle or punish an evil doer. Some persons believe that only a distant and majestic God can inspire worship. They believe that Divine intimacy and personal companionship somehow diminish the divine majesty. They have forgotten that love and not power ultimately define God's relationship to humankind.

But, the Celtic spiritual teachers and today's process-relational Christians see intimacy and love as the true center of God's relationship to the universe. The God of intimate presence is the "Holy Here." Though each moment is unique in the whole universe, all moments arise from the One who lives and moves through all things and in all things. This all-encompassing God who draws circles around each moment is also "Wholly Here," bringing beauty and healing in their fullness to each moment of experience and every aspect of our lives. As the prophet Isaiah discovered, all things are "full" of God's glory! (Isaiah 6:3)

The Healer from Nazareth lived this truth. Jesus saw each person as a reflection of the divine light from whom all life emerges. Just think of Jesus' affirmation of his male and female disciples, and his affirmation of you!

> You are the light of the world. A city built on a hill cannot be hid. No one after lighting a lamp puts it under a bushel basket, but on the lampstand, and it gives light to all in the house. In the same way, let your light shine before others, so that they may see your good works, and give glory to your Father in heaven. (Matthew 5:14-16)

What does it mean for you to affirm that "you are the light of the world?" I believe this affirmation proclaims that God's light shines in and through you, giving birth to your unique gifts. God's light lures you forward by the unique vision of beauty and love that only you can incarnate. The One who said "I am the light of the world" calls us each by name and reveals our true identity as God's "lights" in the world. Listen! God is speaking to you. Let God call you by your true name. Let God's voice speak through your voice with a resounding "yes" to your unique life, gifts, and beauty. For you – and everyone you encounter - are cosmic stardust, manifestations of the eternal light of the universe, dynamically embodied in the moment by moment adventures of a small child, a euphoric teenager, an adult struggling to find guidance in midlife, and an elder with Alzheimer's disease.

The Celtic spiritual guides, like true mystics from every time and place, knew that the fullness of God was always more than humans can describe or imagine. The One who births forth universe upon universe dwarfs our imagination and language, both scientific and religious. And, though the Celtic mystics grounded their faith in everyday wonder, they also affirmed the spiritual awareness that transcends words or images. This is the *apophatic* way that identifies God with the dazzling darkness and deep mystery that no being can completely fathom. With humble hearts and minds, we confess that the Holy Adventure always breaks through our doctrines and institutions. With the Hebraic teachers, we affirm that "no one can see God and live." As Augustine of Hippo is reputed to have said, "if you think you fully know it, it isn't God." Intimately present, nevertheless, God is always the Great Beyond. Like the Aslan of C.S. Lewis' *Chronicles of Narnia*, the Holy One is not tame.

Still, the Celtic mystics knew that God's spirit breathed through all things, giving life and guidance, and bringing forth beauty and love. For God is also the "Beyond Within." God blesses us in every step and encounter. All places are thin places and all persons are thin persons, even though ignorance and pain often disguise God's presence.

All things reveal the divine. All things conceal the divine. All things play their unique role in the Divine Adventure which is at once God's and our own. The God within you is awesome wonder and gives birth to the wonder of your own being. As a poster says, "all the wonders you seek are within yourself." But, how easily these wonders are concealed in our own lives! In the film "The Lion King," the great king's son has lost his way. He no longer knows who he is or the nature of his life's destiny. Paralyzed by fear, he sees himself as a failure, unworthy to bear the weight of his race and save them from their plight. But, when his mentor leads him to the banks of the river and shows him his reflection, he finally discovers the greatness of his true nature mirrored in the water's surface. As he looks at his reflection in the river, all he sees at first is a frightened and impotent lion, quaking at the slightest breeze. But, then, as he looks deeper, he sees the growing reflection of his father, the Great King, and discovers his true identity as the Great King for his own time, the bold savior of his community right now.

Each of us has power and insight beyond our imaginations. Jesus tells each of us, "You are the light of the world." God's wonders stream through you with your every breath. God speaks to you each moment in sighs too deep for words. In each moment, we have all the wisdom and courage we need to humbly journey forward one step at a time. In each moment, divine possibility lures us forward on an adventure of self-discovery and planetary transformation. We are interdependent cells in our planet's life, and the health and well being of the planet depends on our own wholeness and well being. We are all part of the "body of Christ," irreplaceable and essential to the health of our families, communities, congregations, and the planet. (I

Corinthians 4:27)

As they crossed dangerous frontiers or sailed into unknown seas, the Celtic adventurers knew that God guided them by starlight and sunlight, by breezes and portents, and by their own inner wisdom. Threatened by storms and political opponents, they often lost their nerve. But, amid the storm, new courage was born as these adventurers discovered their true stature and courage. They realized that nothing could separate them from God's love, because divine love was their deepest reality and protection. The One who stilled the storm at sea was their closest companion and spiritual guide. By Christ's presence in their lives, they experienced peace amid the inner and outer storms of life, for God is Wholly Here.

YOU ARE CREATED IN GOD'S IMAGE

Creation-affirming mystics such as Meister Eckhardt, Hildegaard of Bingen, and Julian of Norwich join the Celtic adventurers in reminding us that all creatures are words of God. You are a word of God, a unique manifestation of the divine melody. You are created in original wholeness. At your conception, God blessed you with everlasting life. God pronounced you very good and you can never lose that primordial blessing that the Holy One not only gave to Jesus at his baptism, but also gives to each human being:

You are my beloved daughter in whom I am well pleased.
You are my beloved son in whom I well pleased. (Matthew 3:17)

45

In the deep mystery of Divine Creativity whose love brings forth all things, the Creative One spoke these words of humankind. The Lover of All Things spoke these words about you:

> Let us make humankind in our image and likeness....
> So God created humankind in the divine image,
> In the image of the Divine, God created them,
> Male and Female God created them.
> And God blessed them, and said to them, "Be fruitful and
> multiply."
> And God saw everything that God had made, and indeed, it
> was very good. (Genesis 1:26a, 27-28a, 31)

The All Centering and Encompassing Creative Adventure neither begins nor ends. In each moment, the God's Loving Word radiates forth, creating anew, birthing life and love and beauty, challenging injustice and comforting the troubled. That Holy Word, the same yesterday, today, and tomorrow, says to you:

> I create you in my own image.
> I affirm your gender and sexuality.
> You are very good.
> I bless you in your uniqueness.
> Be fruitful with your life.
> Be abundant in multiplying your gifts.
> Bless others by your own self-affirmation.
> Let your blessings reflect the blessing you receive from me.
> Right now, as you read God's affirmation of your life, can you
> affirm your identity as a child of Creative Intelligence? Can
> you say the following affirmations?
> I am created in God's image.
> As God's creation, I am very good.

All women and men are created in God's image.[14]

Celtic theologians and spiritual guides throughout the centuries proclaim that we are born in grace and not sin. As J. Philip Newell affirms, "every child is conceived and born in the image of God."[15] Although the divine image may be hidden by years of abuse, self-forgetfulness, hatred, and fear, the original wholeness of life always remains. Even those person whom we see as limited, disabled, comatose, or dying, reflect God's original wholeness and beauty.

The traditional doctrine of sin is complex and multifaceted, but what theologians have described by the word "sin" involves both the pride and passivity by which we turn from our true relational center, whose connections tether us equally to God, ourselves, and our neighbor. We are always at the divine center, but our centeredness arises from our recognition that the wellspring of divine love brings forth every other center of experience, that is, every other creature, as well. Original wholeness is reclaimed whenever we remember that our true center is grounded in the Divine Parent who eternally joins us with every other member of God's creation. The Holy One comes into the

---

[14] It is important to honor God in the breadth of sexual diversity, whether in the experience of celibate priests, nuns, and monastics or in the LGBT community and those searching for their authentic sexual and gender identity.

[15] J. Philip Newell, *Listening for the Heartbeat of God: A Celtic Spirituality* (New York: Paulist, 1993), p. 13.

world and our lives not to restore what is irrevocably broken, but to manifest the radiant beauty that is hidden within us and within all loving relationships by injustice, self-centeredness, and forgetfulness.

In the matrix of relationships, God is the ultimate artist and pluralist, prodigally bringing forth diversity and uniqueness. In the spirit of divine abundance, Abraham Joshua Heschel notes that "each of us is an original not a copy." It is important to recognize that without the actualization of our gifts, the universe will not find its completeness. Within the body of Christ, each of our gifts matters in the health of the totality. God speaks through your gifts to bring forth the wonders of others.

YOU ARE A LITTLE CHRIST

The true light that enlightens all things is your deepest reality. The early Christian teacher Paul of Tarsus affirms that the greatest mystery in life is "Christ in you, the hope of glory." (Colossians 1:28) The Celtic spiritual guide Columbanus proclaims, "Live in Christ, Christ lives in you."[16]

Holistic medicine informs us that the mind is present throughout the body. Within the body of Christ, which embraces the universe as a whole as well as particular communities of faith, Christ permeates every organ and cell, every mind and body, every planet and galaxy.

---

[16] Quoted in William Parker Marsh, *Celtic Christianity: Ecology and Holiness* (Sturbridge, MA: Landisfarne Press, 1987), p. 21.

> All things have been created through Christ and for
> Christ. Christ is before all things and in Christ all
> things hold together. (Colossians 1:16-17)

Fully embodied in Jesus of Nazareth, the "mind of Christ," God's Word and Wisdom brings life to all things. But, the Christ of the cosmos is always "more" than we can imagine. Not limited to God's revelation in the Savior and Healer Jesus of Nazareth or the boundaries of the Christian faith, Christ is the universal and intimate wisdom of God, luring all things from within and without toward their true wholeness. Christ's true light, "enlightens all." (John 1:9) Christ is bigger than Christianity, yet as intimate as your next breath.

St. Columba, whose journey brought him over perilous seas from Ireland to the Isle of Iona on the West of Scotland to preach the good news of the Risen One, proclaimed that "Christ is my druid." Christ is the inner teacher and companion of all, even those who do not know the Christ's name. Long before Christianity had arrived on Scotland's shores, Christ was already inspiring the highest aspirations of its native peoples. In the spirit of Celtic thought, Christ is our *anam cara*, the intimate friend of our souls, whose love transforms our experiences of pain and suffering into lives beauty and wonder. Christ mirrors our deepest gifts and gives us the courage to share these gifts in our own Holy Adventure.

The inner Christ – God's *anam cara* - awakens us to become unique reflections of divine wisdom in our concrete worlds. You are a "little Christ," as Protestant Reformer Martin Luther proclaims, whose calling in your own holy adventure is to share the boundless love you have received.

Although uniquely complete in his incarnation of the God's wisdom and love, the healer of Nazareth calls each of us to become healers, sharing God's light and love by touch, word, and deed.

The apostle Paul called this experience having "the mind of Christ," which enables us to see our unity with all things and bring forth the mind and heart of Christ in another through our own sacrificial love. (Philippians 2:5-11) In Christ, we are channels of the ever flowing grace whose love awakens the Holy Adventure in everything we touch. In Christ, we are saved and transformed and, then, transform one another, not by coercive power but caring, affirmative, and sacrificial relationships, grounded in our own awareness of God's love for us.

YOU ARE A BARD OF THE HOLY GHOST

Nearly two hundred years ago, Ralph Waldo Emerson was branded a heretic after addressing the students of the Harvard Divinity School with the words, "you are a bard of the Holy Ghost." Your life is a hymn, a melody, a chant, a rap, a praise, so proclaims the wisdom of Celtic spirituality and process theology.

Welling up from the depths of the unconscious, from the primal melody of creation that joins all things, our own unique voices spring forth. Your voice and your life, is an echo of divine wisdom. Regardless of your range, your voice is beautiful!

Within the context of our lives and our own unique gifts, we each have a song to sing. We are meant to harmonize with others. But, the harmony itself depends on our claiming our own voice and singing our own song. Do you remember the story of the Queen Esther? When her people were threatened with annihilation, Esther, spoke up "for just such a time as this." For years, she had hidden her Hebraic identity in order to avoid conflict and gain the king's favor. But, now she must claim her own voice, regardless of the personal cost, to save her people. When she sang her truth, her people were saved.

What is your true voice? What is the melody of your soul? What is the gift that only you can bring to the melody of cosmic creation? What is the unique vibration that animates your spirit as it radiates from your heart across the universe?

Listen! Let God sing within your songs. Perhaps, it is simply a song of gratitude or wonder, or a shout of joy, or the words of a tongue that no one but you and God can understand. Chant the melody of creation with the One who rejoices in the lilt of each voice.

YOUR BODY IS THE TEMPLE OF GOD

The Celtic philosopher Johns Scotus Eriugena proclaimed that the body is the echo of the soul. He affirmed that just as the soul is the image of God, the body is the image of the soul. Though his orthodoxy was also questioned by those who scorned the flesh, John Scotus was simply affirming the great truth of the Incarnation, "the word was made flesh and lived among us, full of grace and truth," embodied in the Jewish baby Jesus. (John 1:14) God sees the world from the vantage point of a manger, a cross, and an empty tomb, and through the perspective of our own eyes as well.

God loves the world. God loves mountains, pine trees, moose and bear, wild flowers, and human artifacts. God loves the body in all its many manifestations – feasting and fasting, running and resting, conceiving and dying. God loves the feel of your skin and the texture of your face. Each wrinkle is caressed by God's holy touch. The radical truth of scripture is that in some mysterious way, God has a body, though not a physical or human body. God is embodied in the world of human flesh – in Jesus of Nazareth but also in all nature, the birds of the air and the beasts of the land and sea. We are all part of the body of Christ, the God-breathed world in whom we live, move, and have our being.

Often disguised by our adherence our culture's norms of physical perfection, we forget that our bodies are also a reflection of God's original wholeness. Do you recall Paul of Tarsus' affirmation?

> Do you not know that your body is the temple of the Holy Spirit within you, which you have from God and that you are not your own. For you were bought with a price; therefore glorify God in your body. (I Corinthians 5:19-20)

Awakened to the wonders of the incarnation, the Holy One invites you to love God in your body. Give thanks to God by your eating and drinking. Praise God in sexuality and touch. Love God in your embodiment and senses. Feel the love God in the touch of your child, the skin of your beloved, the face of your soul friend. Rejoice in the abundant variety all of the Divine Artist's colors and sizes.

Tragically, for many of us, the body is perceived as the primary revelation of what some have called "original sin." We see ourselves as ugly and deformed. We look enviously at bodies that are younger, more muscular, thinner, and glamorous than our own and fail to honor our own unique revelation of the Creator. Our bodies have been abused, misused, and mocked. Their wholeness maligned and degraded. Out of our own body denial and fear, we judge other bodies – objectifying them as vehicles of lust or scorn. Fearing their own sexuality, some spiritual leaders deny their own flesh and project their evil passions on other bodies as "occasions of sin." Yet, as Celtic theologian and spiritual guide Philip Newell notes, "your body is a sacred text."[17] The body, male and female in all its expressions, is loved by God and mirrors the divine creativity. Male and female, young and old, our bodies are "occasions of love," creativity, and unity. The Heart of the Universe embraces and soothes you.

Within the body of Christ, each cell is alive,

---

[17] J. Philip Newell, *Echo of the Soul* (Harrisburg: Morehouse, 2000), p. xviii.

beloved, and full of grace. Body, mind, and spirit interpenetrate one another, bringing forth the enchantment of sense and thought and soul. The mind, emotions, and spirit shape the body, just as the body shapes the mind and spirit, in an eternal harmony. Even brokenness and pain reveal the essential partnership of spirit and flesh, and the Divine Beauty that animates all flesh.

Your body is the temple of the Spirit, a shrine where the infinite and finite are united. The body is an icon which can awaken us to beauties beyond our imagination. Holy love of the flesh inspires a true Platonic love in which the beauty of each body reminds us of the Eternal Beauty that is our origin and destiny.

So, glorify God in your body. Moving throughout every cell and galaxy, every human and animal, is the Divine impulse toward wholeness. Without a deep inner urge toward healing and wholeness, we would never recover from the most superficial wound, a broken leg, cancer, or heart disease. This healing impulse mends broken hearts, comforts the grieving, and companions the dying.

In my own spiritual pilgrimage, this urge toward healing is manifest most fully in the spiritual companionship of Jesus of Nazareth, who brought healing to every encounter - by touch, word, hospitality, challenge, and openness to the other's pain. The healer of Nazareth empowers each of us to be healers in our time and place, beginning with our own sacred flesh and embracing the holiness of others. God's impulse of light and love flowed through Jesus and now it flows through you. Your touch can heal the sick and comfort the hurting. You can be a channel of wholeness simply by letting God's light flow from you to the one beside you.[18]

It is not an understatement to say that our lives are sensational. Moment by moment we are awakened to beauty and wonder by our many senses. The heavens declare the glory of God and so do the hairs in our nose and the taste buds on our tongue. The Christ within us guides us toward the path of wholeness for ourselves and others. Our touch brings healing to others. Reflecting the healing impulse, we may become the unexpected healers and answers to the prayers of persons in need. When we share food, seek justice, touch brokenness, and soothe pain, we say "yes" to the God's Healing Adventure that flows through our lives.

You are both the center and an ever-moving circumference of God's love and light. You are God's image, Christ's companion, and the Spirit's voice. You are cosmic stardust, awesome wonder, amazing grace, and surprising beauty.

---

[18] For a reflection on the relationship of spirituality and healing, see Bruce Epperly, *Spirituality and Health, Health and Spirituality* (Mystic, CT: Twenty Third Publications, 1997) ; *God's Touch: Faith, Wholeness, and the Healing Miracles of Jesus* (Louisville: Westminster/John Knox, 2001); and *Healing Worship: Purpose and Practice* (Cleveland: Pilgrim Press, 2006).

PRAYERS FOR THE PILGRIMAGE

Exercise One - Finding your circle of quiet. Feminist spiritual guide and theologian Nelle Morton affirms that we hear each other into speaking our own voices. Oddly enough, we all too often listen to other's voices rather than our own. We assume that others know the tune, while neglect to seek our own voice. Still, heard or not, God's voice speaks through us, patiently waiting for us to listen and sing.

We can discern our true voice in many ways, the simplest of which is through stillness. Take time to relax in God's presence, opening to the divine wisdom speaking through your own experience. Listen to your life in quiet moments. Let the many voices bubble up to the surface without judgment as you open to the "sighs too deep for words."

God's inner voice, animating your true word, may come as a quiet word, an image or icon, a challenge, or lure toward something unexpected. But, in the stillness, you will find healing and direction. You will discover your song!

Exercise Two – Using Your Healing Imagination. We can also discover our true voice through practicing meditative visualizations. In this prayer for the pilgrimage, breathe deeply the quiet presence of God until you feel a sense of calm centeredness. Now, as you breathe, feel the divine light entering you as well as welling up from you. Let your heart, mind, lungs, and whole being fill with holy and healing light. Where there is disease of mind, body, spirit, or relationships, let the light permeate and heal that discomfort or pain. Experience the light surrounding you so that you will be guided and protected by the light. In the Circle of God's light, you can claim your unique gifts, the voice that is yours alone, without fear.

Life is a constant process of de-centering and re-centering, especially as we explore the circumferences of our experience. Amid the challenges of work, relationships, and self-discovery, we often temporarily "lose our center" and forget our voice. But, in fact, we can never fully lose our center, even when we imitate another or forget our truth in conflict and chaos. The Center holds even as the circumference moves. In quiet moments, we rediscover that we are at the center of Divine Love and that this center embraces all things.

Exercise Three - Finding the Christ Within. In quiet, let go of the challenges of past, present, and future. Take a few minutes to simply rest in God's presence as you listen for God's voice in your life. Imagine yourself in a place of beauty. What do the surroundings look like? How does it feel to be in this place of beauty, wonder, and safety? Is it breezy and warm, or cool and still? What are the textures around you?

In the quiet of the place, visualize yourself having a conversation with the Living Christ. How do you visualize the Living Christ? Christ engages you in a conversation. What does the Christ say to you? What words do you share with the Christ?

In the course of your conversation, Christ reminds you of his (or her) presence with words such as these, "I am everywhere. But, I am also within you. Seek me within and you will find me." See the Christ intimately growing within your heart. What does Christ look like there?

Take time to search for the "little Christ" in your heart. What images do you have of your own inner Christ? What gifts of Christ are uniquely yours? In what ways will you share these gifts with others? Claim your own inner Christ.

As you conclude this meditation, remember that Christ is always with you, whether you image Christ or not, ready to provide the guidance, courage, and love you need for the adventure ahead.

Exercise Four - Becoming a Bard of the Holy Ghost. God's voice sings in all things, and God's voice sings in your life. In this meditation, we playfully awaken to God's voice within us. We joyfully claim our place as a bard or poet of the Holy Spirit.

Rest and relax in God's spirit. You may choose to sit, walk, or recline as you do this meditation with an attitude of joyful and attentive playfulness.

In the quiet moment, listen to the many songs within your spirit. Perhaps, they will manifest themselves as favorite religious, popular, or classical pieces. Perhaps, they will simply be unnamed melodies. Listen and enjoy the many melodies of the spirit.

In the process of listening to the melody of the spirit deep within your soul, one tune or verse may speak to your life situation. Listen to this tune: what does the music say to you? If there are words, how do they address your life?

Perhaps, you may choose to hum the tune or sing its words. Don't worry about being on key or whether you remember the words. It's your song after all! Let the words well up as you sit or stand. You may choose to get up and dance to them. Simply enjoy the music of your spirit on this particular day.

Later, you may choose to reflect on these words. What message do they have for you? If you truly followed these words, how would they change your life?

As you look at your life, where do you feel safest in singing these words? With whom would you like to share the melody and words? Visualize yourself singing in harmony with those with whom you share a spiritual melody.

Conclude by giving God thanks for your own unique voice. Affirm God's voice in your life and the lives with whom you share your song.

Exercise Five -Finding your gifts for the world. The Christian spiritual leader Paul of Tarsus claimed that we are part of the body of Christ. Within this holy body, each of us has a unique role. Paul imaged our gifts and lives in terms of organs and body parts. Our gifts radiate across the body, bringing health to the whole organism.

In the quiet, visualize yourself as a member of a beautiful and radiant body. Within this body, streams of life and health are constantly flowing. Each part of the body is constantly being nurtured by a lively Spirit and each part nurtures its neighbors and the whole.

In your mind's eye, visualize yourself as being a part of this dynamic and healthy body. What part are you – an arm, leg, stomach, T-cell, brain, heart, foot? What is significant about your role in the body? How does it reflect your gifts and identity?

Experience the holy light flowing through the body, giving life and health to your particular part. What does it feel like to be permeated by healthy and dynamic energy? Experience your part of the body as healthy and whole. What unique talent do you have for the well being of the whole?

Within the body, what other parts are essential to your well being? Feel your connectedness to the other parts. You may choose to personify these other parts of the body with the images of family members, spouses, friends, and colleagues. Experience the interdependent fabric of life, the unity of the whole and the uniqueness of your part.

In conclusion, take time to express your gratitude to the other body parts for their nurture and support. Take time to thank the Holy Spirit who gives life to the body. Honor your own gift within the totality.

Exercise Six - A Healing Meditation. Jesus of Nazareth was known as the Healer. As an embodiment of God's ever-present Wisdom, Jesus is our soul's friend and intimate companion. Jesus' healings revealed his commitment to wholeness and abundant life for all. This same healing love is alive and active in our world. But, we need to open ourselves to this Divine energy of love to experience our own wholeness and share that wholeness with others.

Visualize yourself in a quiet and safe place, a place of beauty and wonder, where God is present in your life. As you enjoy this "thin place" of divine beauty, you recognize that the Healing Christ is your companion. Visualize the Healing Christ if you are able. In the gentleness of Christ's presence, you hear him ask: "Where do you need to be healed in your life?"

Let the words soak in as you reflect on Christ's question. After a few moments, how do you respond? Where do you need healing? Share with the Christ the depths of your heart. Experience him listening deeply and awakening you to your deepest needs.

After a few more moments, Christ asks again, "Do you want to be healed?" How do you respond to this question?

In the gentleness of conversation with the Friend of your soul, hear Christ ask: "would you like my healing touch?" Reflect on the question. If you choose to say "no," or if you are uncertain or afraid, take time to share your feelings with Christ, listening to Christ's responses, with the knowledge that Christ is always there to transform your life.

If you choose to say "yes," experience Christ touching you. In what way does he touch you? How does it feel to be touched by the Healing Christ? In what ways does this touch change your life? Let Christ's touch transform both your mind and body.

Whether or not you experience anything dramatic, and regardless of your response to Christ's questions, conclude by opening to God's touch in gratitude and trust.

CHAPTER THREE

COMPANIONSHIP ON THE HOLY
ADVENTURE

I arise today
With the might of heaven:
The rays of the sun,
The beams of the moon,
The glory of fire,
The speed of wind,
The depth of sea,
The stability of earth,
The hardness of rock.[20]

From the quiet center, the pilgrim takes her first steps toward an unknown frontier. Each day brings a new adventure. Each encounter is a spiritual challenge. Beyond the path, faeries and leprechauns may play, but deeper in the shadows of the forest lurk goblins and ogres. This is where the wild things are!

Whether they chronicle Patrick escaping the wrath of a local warlord or a young woman milking her cow, the tales of Celtic spirituality abound in adventurous journeys. For those intrepid adventurers, seeking the center meant becoming a peregrine, or pilgrim, whose external journeys mirrored her or his inner spiritual pilgrimage.

The lure of the Holy Adventure inspired Columba, Patrick, and Brendan, to embark upon adventures into unexplored lands.[21] As they launched into deep waters without oar or compass, they trusted that God would lead them to their place of resurrection, that thin and holy place of rebirth and transformation.

These companions of the Spirit lived out their theology as they were buffeted by every wave and each shifting wind. They knew first-hand the meaning of that grand theological term "omnipresence." While armchair adventurers can mouth great spiritual truths, peregrine travelers into vast oceanic unknowns offer wisdom of a different sort – the wisdom of spiritual pioneers who navigate constantly between life and death. To those Celtic pilgrims, God was their true center and God would be with them through all of life's adventures. They saw themselves as "hospes mundi," guests of the world, encircled and blessed by the Holy Adventure. The breast plate of St. Patrick, the Lorica, proclaims the holy enchantment of this God-breathed world.

> Christ behind and before me,
> Christ beneath and above me,
> Christ with me and in me,
> Christ around and about me,
> Christ on my left and on my right
> Christ when I arise in the morning,
> Christ when I lie down at night,
> Christ in each heart that thinks of me,
> Christ in each mouth that speaks of me,
> Christ in each eye that sees me,
> Christ in each ear that hears me.[22]

At the end of the day, when darkness threatens to envelope the glow of his fire and strange cries in the night chill his soul, another traveler remembers that wherever he is, God is his companion. God is so close that, like a loving parent or friend, the Holy Trinity crawls under the blanket to warm and reassure this lonely pilgrim.

> I lie down this night with God,
> And God would lie down with me.
> I lie down this night with Christ,
> And Christ would lie down with me.
> I lie down this night with the Spirit,
> And the Spirit would lie down with me.
> God, Christ, and Spirit,
> Be lying down with me.[23]

As you meditate upon this poem, how would you feel if experienced God as near as your partner sleeping beside you or a child resting in your arms?

God is as intimate as the one lying beside you and as close as your next breath. For these Celtic adventurers, God's Spirit of safety and protection will have the final word for every personal adventure. Often threatened by storms at sea and enemies on land, the intrepid Columba, whose journeys took him from Ireland to Iona and across the stark Scottish wilderness, lived by the life-changing affirmation, "the path I walk, Christ walks."

These ancient travelers knew that even when they had lost heart, a greater heart beat within them. When they did not know the path ahead, they believed that a deeper guide directed their homeward steps. It has been said that there are only two kinds of persons: those who are in God's hands and know it; and those who are in God's hands and don't know it. Our Celtic spiritual parents knew well that they were in God's hands regardless of the external threats that confronted them! They also knew that God calls to action as well as contemplation, and to adventure as well as rest.

The Celtic spiritual guides remind us that, despite the apparent ordinariness of our lives, we are all on an eternal journey with the Holy Adventurer as our companion. Even though our daily sojourns may be in familiar places, the spiritual voyages of Brendan and Columba still chart our journey. Their adventures show us that although the far horizons are a mystery, God always provides light enough for one step at a time.

Can you imagine the challenges of body and spirit that confronted those ancient Hebrew pilgrims, Abraham and Sarah? Lured from their familiar home with the promise that they would become parents of a great nation, this childless couple journeyed into the uncharted wilderness with only a vision and a promise to guide their quest.

We are the spiritual children of Abraham and Sarah, the Celtic pilgrims, and the Native American vision questers. As I looked up from the computer screen on a summer day a few years back, I gazed upon a hoodoo, or chimney rock, emerging from the mountainside adjacent to Ring Lake Ranch. Natural pillars such as the chimney rock captured the imagination of Native Americans and Hebraic travelers. Reaching toward heaven, these natural formations reminded them that God is not limited by space or time. Though our vision of reality is animated by quantum physics and cosmology rather than the three story universe of the ancients, we can still affirm their vision of a Spiritual Companion whose creativity breathes life into infants and rock formations and makes all things thin places of revelation and healing. For those who follow the paths of the Holy Adventure, each place is a holy place and each step is a journey into God. As you look at your own life, to what great adventure is God calling?

While the First American seekers honored the natural stone pillars as they found them, Abraham and Sarah erected their own "hoodoo" or "Ebenezer," a holy pile of rocks to awaken them to the Divine Presence at each camp site. In an age in which gods were limited by time and space, the God who blessed their home was also the guardian of unfamiliar paths. At such spots, they may have imagined themselves invoking the Holy One, when, in fact, God was already invoking them, and challenging to believe that wherever they went, they were encompassed by the Holy One. In those wilderness places, where the familiar and unfamiliar meet and we find ourselves at the edges of our known universe, we can affirm that the Holy Adventure who guided Abraham, Sarah, and the Native American visionaries also guides our steps.

Years later, jealous that Hagar's son Ishmael might supplant her own son Isaac as heir to the family fortune, Sarah demands that Abraham banish Hagar and her son Ishmael into the wilderness. Weary and dying of thirst,

Hagar cries out to the Holy One to save Ishmael and discovers that even the parched desert is a thin and verdant place, where miracles can deliver the lost and forsaken. In the stillness, Hagar hears an angelic voice that leads her into her own spiritual promised land.

> "Do not be afraid; for God has heard the voice of the boy where he is. Come, lift up the boy, and hold him fast with your hand, for I will make a nation of him." Then God opened her eyes and she saw a well of water. She went and filled the skin with water, and gave the boy a drink. (Genesis 21:17-20)

There are times when a vision quest is thrust upon us. Complacent with our predictable lives, we are thrown into the wilderness of uncertainty by a medical diagnosis, marital crisis, financial upheaval, emotional disturbance, or job loss. The enveloping wilderness is filled with strange beasts and overwhelming fears. Apocalyptic thinking dominates us as death, failure, loneliness, and chaos loom on the horizon. In the midst of the chaos, a quiet voice summons us back to awareness, "Do not be afraid. I am with you. I will guide your steps." The center holds, the circle encompasses us, and we find a path through the wilderness.

When my position as Protestant Chaplain at Georgetown University was eliminated in 1999 after nearly twenty years of service, I was thrust into a vocational and spiritual wilderness. All my prior certainties collapsed. My vision of a stable and predictable future shattered. Fearful and depressed, I kept asking myself "now what?" Though the future was uncertain and filled with vocational and financial anxiety, I found hope in two great spiritual promises:

"Nothing can separate me from the love of God."
(Romans 8:39)

"For surely I know the plans I have for you, says the Lord, plans for your welfare and not your harm, to give you a future and a hope." (Jeremiah 29:11)

God had a vision for my "new" future that would include unimagined possibilities as I took the first steps toward a novel professional horizon. These same promises sustained me, when our son Matt was diagnosed with cancer. We walked an uncertain path, with only one certainty, the great faithfulness of God that gives us life in the midst of death. We see God's promise of new life in the smile of our six month old grandson. Today, I begin a new spiritual and professional adventure as I conclude nearly eight years at Lancaster Theological Seminary. With my position eliminated due to seminary finances and restructuring, I experience both the insecurity and excitement of emerging possibilities. But, despite my anxiety, I trust that God is with me supplying visions and energy to achieve them just as God did in our son's hospital room and eleven years ago, when my position was eliminated at Georgetown University.

Alone and fearful about the future, we discover the meaning of another great theological word - "divine omniscience." This ancient doctrine affirms simply that: I am known and loved wherever I am, and regardless of where I may journey. The One who knows me guides me toward a hopeful future even when I cannot see the next step.

The Psalms are not for the faint-hearted. Reading them can transform your life. The Psalms emerged out of political intrigues and personal conflicts. They embrace both celebration and lamentation, and affirm that when confidence in our own resources and the support of others is shaken, a well spring of inspiration and confidence eventually bursts forth. Thinking ourselves God-forsaken, we discover the Companion who has quietly carried and guided us through the toughest times.

> Where can I go from your spirit?
> And where can I flee from your presence?
> If I ascend to heaven, you are there.
> If I take the wings of the morning and settle at the farthest
>   limits of the sea,
> Even there your hand shall lead me,
> And your right hand shall hold me fast.
> If I say, "Surely darkness shall cover me, and the light
>   around me become night,
> Even the darkness is not dark to you;
> The night is as bright as the day,
> For darkness is as light to you.
>   (Psalm 139:7-12)

God is always watching over us. More than that, God knows us from the inside out. As contemporary theologians assert, "God is in all things and all things are in God." And, God's knowledge of us, in all the complexity of our lives, only adds to God's love for us. Living from the divine center, we live by healing and empowering affirmations of faith:

> God knows me and loves me.
> God is with me wherever I go.
> God will lead me through the darkness.
> God's light guides me even when I feel lost.

As a parent of a child diagnosed with a life-defining cancer, I found comfort knowing that God experienced our pain and uncertainty, and that although God did not cause the cancer, God worked within the healing forces in our son's body, our prayers and healing touch, the wisdom of his oncologist and her colleagues, and the strange curative powers of chemotherapy. I knew that God felt my tears and anxiety, and that God also experienced my celebration as medical tests confirmed the likelihood of a cure, the gift of the intricate combination of meditation and medication, reiki healing touch and our prayers and the prayers of our friends, and the mysterious powers of chemical agents that sustain life by their toxicity.

MANURE ON THE LABYRINTH

I am a labyrinth walker. Wherever I go, I seek out the deep wisdom of these circles of healing and transformation. The gentle path of the labyrinth reminds me that however circuitous the journey may be, there is always a center to lure us forward and bring us home. One morning as I walked the Ring Lake labyrinth, contemplating the next steps in my own personal journey,

I found myself enthralled by the shimmering lake and the majestic vista. I rejoiced in the beauty of everything I saw. But, as looked down, I noticed that the free ranging horses had left an offering on the labyrinth. I was ankle deep in green spirituality! Manure is part of the spiritual pilgrimage. Manure can soil a pair of shoes. It can also fertilize a garden and nurture a growing pine tree or awaken an absent-minded theologian to the multi-dimensional nature of life.

Buddhist teachers remind us that before we are enlightened, we chop wood and carry water. With the liberating vision of *satori*, or enlightenment, we continue to chop wood and carry water, but now we perform these mundane tasks from the perspective of enlightenment. Manure is as much a part of the spiritual pilgrimage as revelatory experiences. Epiphanies are heralded with exclamations of wonder and surprise. God's glory is revealed in folding the laundry, booting up the computer, and putting on a pair of old shoes. God is in the details of ordinary life, but God is also in the manure – the unexpected and often unwanted moments that soil our images of personal, relational, or vocational perfection. Even ankle deep in manure, we can glimpse the beautiful life God has planned for us.

> With beauty all around me, I walk.
> With Christ as my companion, I walk.
> With manure on my pathway, I walk.
> With the Cross before me, I walk.
> With the Easter on the horizon, I walk.

WHEREVER YOU GO, GOD IS WITH YOU

Imagine the pilgrimage of Mary and Joseph. Without warning, a young girl finds herself to be a thin place for an adventure in holy obstetrics. She is told that her virgin womb will be the home of the Savior of her people. With no prior preparation or warning, Joseph discovers his own thin place, when an angelic visitor calls him to be the protector of this surprising child of God. But, the couple must not linger where they are. In the wake of divine revelation comes the threat of destruction and a hurried flight to a foreign land. The forces of evil ready themselves to destroy the Innocent Child, but the Divine Dream provides a path to safety and place of refuge.

For Celtic Christians, neither the circle nor the cross by itself can fully encompass the spiritual journey. Death and destruction mark every day, and often strike without warning. Around every corner lurks a banshee or a troll. Even the life-changing moments of creative transformation require jettisoning the comfortable past. The circle of life involves birth and death, threat and safety, disorientation and new orientation, the heavens above and manure-scuffed shoes below. But, beyond the death is the promise of resurrection. The circle of God-breathed life radiates into eternity.

St. Patrick knew the importance of finding a spiritual path that embraced darkness and light. Sold into slavery as a child, Patrick eventually gained his freedom and became a champion of the Encompassing Christ. Still, at every bend of the path, enemies lay in wait – the external enemies mirroring his internal uncertainties.

The Lorica, the Breastplate of St. Patrick, arose as prayer of protection for all spiritual travelers. According to legend, a pagan chieftain sought to kill St. Patrick. A band of mercenaries drew close to the unarmed pilgrim, but were confounded when Patrick escaped their grasp. All they heard on the path way was the cry of a deer running through the thicket. Encircled by divine protection, we – like Patrick -can claim the Safe Center that holds despite the threat.

> I arise today
> Through a mighty strength, the invocation of the Trinity,
> Through belief in the threeness,
> Through confession of the oneness
> Of the Creator of Creation.
> I arise today
> Through the strength of Christ's birth with his baptism,
> Through the strength of his crucifixion with his burial,
> Through the strength of his resurrection with his ascension,
> Through the strength of his descent for the judgment of
> Doom....
> I arise today
> Through God's strength to pilot me:
> God's might to uphold me,
> God's hand to guard me,
> God's shield to protect me,
> God's ear to hear me,
> God's host to save me,
> From the snare of devils,
> From temptation of vices,
> From all who shall wish me ill,
> Afar and anear,
> Alone and in a multitude.[19]

---

[19] Esther de Waal, *Every Earthly Blessing*, p. xxi.

Christ our *anam cara*, or closest spiritual companion, travels the path with us. His own suffering and triumph join the cross and the circle. Jesus' death gives us hope that in the midst of peril we are known, loved, and protected. The Holy Caim, the Divine Circle, claims darkness and light, death and light, conflict and reconciliation, as holy ground. Christ's revelation declares that, despite the threats that abound in our lives, God's love is stronger than death. Light transforms darkness into the womb of creativity. Perpetual perishing gives birth to Eternity.

Pondering his own death and the martyrdom of his dearest friends, Paul of Tarsus, another peregrine of Christ, inscribes his own spiritual breastplate with words of divine protection:

> Who will separate us from the love of Christ? Will hardship, or distress, or persecution, or famine, or nakedness, or peril, or sword?.... No, in all these things, we are more than conquerors through him who loved us. For I am convinced that neither death, nor life, nor angels, nor rulers, nor things present, nor things to come, nor powers, nor height, nor depth, nor anything else in all creation, will be able to separate us from the love of God in Christ Jesus our Lord. (Romans 8:35, 37-39)

Our deepest fears become our greatest strengths when we place them in the Divine Center.

A JOURNEY WITHOUT DISTANCE

Feminist spiritual guide Nelle Morton noted that "the journey is home." Our spiritual pilgrimages often take place in turbulent waters and unfamiliar places. But, our journeys are also lived out in daily interactions with our families and co-workers.

All places are thin places. All encounters are epiphanies. Mary of Bethany may sit contemplatively for hours at the feet of the teacher Jesus, but eventually she must help Martha with the dishes. Martha cleans and cooks, but she must also find holiness in the clutter as well as in intimate Sabbath moments with Jesus. The morning after his homecoming celebration, the prodigal son must go back to work in his father's business.

The Celtic tradition celebrated the ordinary. The word was made flesh and dwells among us in kindling the fire, milking the cow, or preparing for a trip to the market. The whole earth is full of God's glory and so are the fireplace and the barn. When the teacher Diarchellach was planning a pilgrimage, the spiritual guide Samhthann challenged him, "If God could not be found on this side of the sea we would indeed journey across. Since, however, God is nigh unto all who call upon [the Divine], we are under no obligation to cross the sea. The kingdom of heaven can be reached from every land."[20]

This moment is the moment of salvation and healing. This place gives birth to divine revelation. The birds of the air, the children on the way to the bus stop, the

---

[20] *Living Between Two Worlds*, p. 60.

co-workers at the water cooler show us the way to our own thin places. As the Celts knew, all acts – even the most ordinary domestic chores - are done on holy ground when we recognize that God is our partner. As one Celtic homemaker affirmed:

> This morning, as I kindle the fire upon my hearth, I pray that the flame of God's love may burn in my heart, and the hearts of all I meet today. I pray that no envy and malice, no hatred or fear, my smother the flame. I pray that indifference and apathy, contempt and pride, may not pour like cold water on the fire. Instead, may the spark of God's love light the love in my heart, that it may burn brightly through the day.
>
> And may I warm those that are lonely, whose hearts are cold and lifeless, So that all may know the comfort of God's love.[21]

Traditional Celtic spirituality prescribes the daily "blessing of the hands," the conscious commitment to perform each task for the glory of God and the well being of creation. What we do really matters. Our actions radiate across our households and across the universe. An act of kindness can change the course of a human life and the history of the planet. Our lives are our gifts to God, whose own journey embraces all things. More important than lifeless doctrinal orthodoxy is the love that welcomes, affirms, and heals. For those with eyes to see, God speaks through every encounter and every task. We are partners and co-creators with God in bringing beauty to the microcosm and the

---

[21] de Weyer, *Celtic Fire,* p. 77.

macrocosm. The One who loved the lilies of the field, the birds of the air, and small children takes delight in the ordinary affairs of life. Our common acts support God's own healing of the earth.

> Come, Mary, and milk my cow,
> Come, Bride, and encompass her,
> Come, Columba the benign
> And twine thine arm around my cow.
> Come, Mary Virgin, to my cow,
> Come, great Bride, the beauteous,
> Come, thou milk maid of Jesus Christ,
> And place thine arms beneath my cow.[22]

For those who remember God is here, now, and everywhere, every act is a prayer, every greeting a blessing, and every task a holy adventure. Nothing is commonplace, even milking a cow, when God is your companion. Nothing is unnoticed by the one to whom all hearts are open and all desires known.

> Bless O God my little cow
> Bless O God my desire;
> Bless Thou my partnership
> And the milking of my hands, O God.
> Bless O God each teat
> Bless O God each finger;
> Bless Thou each drop
> That goes into my pitcher, O God.[23]

---

[22] de Waal, *Every Earthly Blessing,* p. 5.

[23] p. 5.

Centered in God's abundant creativity, each day is a holy adventure and each person a hero or heroine on an amazing pilgrimage. We read scripture, biography, autobiography, and fiction to feast on great thoughts and exemplary persons. But, such reading fails in its task if we forget our own unique journey. The thin places of scripture point us to the thin places in our own lives.

Look at a day in your own life. Amid quotidian tasks at home or at the office, you constantly choose for and against life and love. You can add or subtract love from the world's beauty by your thoughts and actions. You can witness to holiness or betray life's goodness by each deed. Ponder the unique wonder of your own life. Singular in the whole universe, you are given the task of transforming yourself and bringing beauty to the lives of others. There are no ordinary tasks when God is your guide and companion.

As Gerard Manley Hopkins proclaimed, "the world is charged with the grandeur of God." All is wonder and miracle. Dugall MacAulay told Alexander Carmichael, the compiler of the compendium of Celtic verse *The Carmina Gadelica,* that he sung this hymn each day upon leaving his house for work.

> God bless to me this day,
> God bless to me this night;
> Bless, O Bless, Thou God of grace,
> Each day and hour of my life;
> Bless, O Bless, Thou God of grace,
> Each day and hour of my life.
> God bless the pathway on which I go,
> God bless the earth that is beneath my sole;
> Bless, O God, and give to me Thy love,

O God of Gods, bless my rest and my repose;
Bless, O God, and give to me Thy love,
And bless, O God of gods, my repose.[24]

From morning to night, we live, move, and have our being in the Divine Center. Think of your own daily prayers of blessing and holiness. Think of the blessings strewn through the most ordinary day. As I turn on the computer each morning to check my e-mail, add a note on Facebook, or begin working on a text, I draw a circle and make the sign of the cross around my workspace as I recite the prayer of the Psalmist,

Let the words of my mouth
And the meditations of my heart
Be acceptable in thy sight
O God, my rock and my salvation.

As a seminary professor, I see my task as a divine calling. My classroom is a moving tabernacle, constructed on holy ground. Before each session, I encircle the class with the light of Christ and open myself to Divine Wisdom. Often I bless the four corners of the room upon entry as a means of committing the hour to God's glory. I envisage each student surrounded and permeated by the light of Christ as I affirm:

God of love and wisdom
Let my teaching illumine my students
Let me hear their deepest voices
And see your presence in each one.

---

[24] de Waal, *The Celtic Way of Prayer*, p. 90.

I believe that my students learn with greater passion and work with greater insight and effectiveness because they know they are blessed and that their work is part of a Greater Adventure, which radiates from the classroom across the world.

Family life is a series of comings and goings. Each morning when I bid my wife good bye as I leave to give a sermon or talk in a neighboring town or catch a flight to a give retreat or lecture across the country, I encircle her in light in the spirit of Celtic encompassing and affirm God's presence with her.

> God guide and protect my Kate
> Give her love and beauty today
> May our love be joined throughout this day

We are subtly joined in God's spirit regardless of the distance that lies between us. Daily, I circle in prayer our son, his wife, and our infant grandson, my closest spiritual friend, and persons in need of divine healing.

For many years, random calls from phone solicitors were a source of annoyance to me, until I realized that it takes more spiritual energy to be rude than to be loving toward them. When the phone rings, I let its ring call me to the simple prayer that "I give Christ's love to the person on the other end of the line," regardless of whom it is. While I seldom purchase anything over the phone, I speak gently and with care, often leaving the solicitor with a blessing. I recognize that, amid the many negative responses that phone solicitors receive, I want to treat each one as a center of Divine Care.

A good friend prays for her children as they cross

the street to catch the school bus. Throughout the day, she encircles them in the light of wisdom and protection. She welcomes them home with snacks and spiritual thoughts.

Another friend images each person who will join her at the dinner table as surrounded by the transforming light of God. Chopping vegetables and cooking rice, she opens her heart to the Divinity in each one. For my friend, preparing food is a profound spiritual discipline -an act of prayerful connectedness and blessing.

The workplace is holy ground. Our beliefs, integrity, patience, and love are put to the test on a daily basis. We are tempted to compartmentalize our lives, reserving one ethical standard for our friends and family, and another for our colleagues and business affairs. At the workplace, we are surrounded by strange beasts and alluring temptations. In the ecology of life, decisions at the workplace can become a matter of life and death for persons we will never meet. We can truly gain the world and lose our souls when we act as if business and government are beyond the boundaries of divine care. But, with one Celtic pilgrim we can pray the hours of our work day.

> Bless to me, O God,
> Each thing mine eye sees;
> Bless to me, O God,
> Each thing my ear hears;
> Bless to me, O God,
> Each odor that goes to my nostrils;
> Bless to me, O God,
> Each taste that goes to my lips;
> Each note that goes to my song,
> Each ray that guides my way,

Each thing that I pursue,
Each lure that tempts my will,
The zeal that seeks my living soul,
The Three that seek my heart,
The zeal that seeks my living soul,
The Three that seek my heart.[25]

A business leader I know begins each day by closing his door and silently praying for the day ahead. As he looks at his calendar, he blesses each meeting. He says a brief prayer as he checks his e-mail and welcomes his secretary. He consciously chooses to see God's presence in each of the women and men who work under his supervision as well as those with whom he does business. Throughout the day he reminds himself that his primary goal is not just to make a profit, but also to serve God by creating a healthy work environment, treating his employees with respect, making an excellent product, and dealing honestly with everyone he meets. He understands that the primary venues for his spiritual growth are his business and home. His secretary often surprises employees and business associates by telling them that he is spending the lunch hour with his wife or has left early for a dance recital or little league game with his grandchildren. Recognizing that his own business practices shape the spiritual lives of his employees, he provides regular wellness and stress reduction programs at the office, allows for liberal leave time for family illness and life celebrations, and allows his employees to devote a percentage of their time to volunteering in the community. His office has become a temple of the spirit, nurturing

---

[25] Esther de Waal, editor, *The Celtic Vision,* p. 6.

employees and clients alike.

In a world of dynamic interrelatedness, our own spiritual commitments and interpersonal actions shape not only our immediate environment but the health of the community and the planet. While it is true that we "act locally and think globally," the "butterfly effect" of chaos theory reminds us that even the smallest act can have global implications. We can choose to be God's companions in healing the world one act at a time.

ALL TIMES ARE HOLY TIMES

We are on a protean adventure with a Shape-shifting God. The Divine Center is lively, vital, and evolutionary. We are most like the Divine when we awaken to our own gifts of creative transformation.

Early Christian thinkers believed that by living through all the stages of life from birth to death, Jesus made each stage of life holy. They affirmed that our task from infancy to death was to become as Christ-like as possible. By loving God in the world of the flesh, our own lives incarnate Divinity in the midst of time.

All places are thin places; all times are holy times. In the Greek language, time is described in terms of *chronos* and *kairos*. *Chronos* time mirrors the ticking of the clock and impending dead lines. Linear in nature it has a distinct beginning and end. Defined by watches and hour glasses, *chronos* time is always slipping away from us. As the terminus point of life's journey, death is foreboding.

Kairos time is marked by holidays and special occasions. *Kairos* is the time of seasons and circles, of that which has neither beginning nor end. *Kairos* moments open the door to the Everlasting Now in which perpetual perishing is woven together with divine steadfastness.[26] Living in *kairos* time, life is abundant, full, and never-ending. There is a time and a season for everything, for time reveals the marriage of eternal wisdom and holy embodiment. The hands of the clock and the changing seasons join tradition and novelty with the surprising spaciousness of the open future. God is alive in each moment and each moment God gives birth to the Christ child.

Often on a car ride, impatient children will ask, "Are we there yet?" A similar spirit is captured by the bumper sticker that asks, "Are we having fun yet?" In the Holy Adventure, life is a pilgrimage in which each moment is sufficient and each step an encounter with the Divine. We are always in the Holy Here. For those whose senses mirror the divine, all times are *kairos* times. With the Psalmist, we proclaim "this is the day that God has made and we will rejoice and be glad in it." (Psalm 118:24)

All ages of life reveal the divine and are lived out within the infinite circumference of God's love. In contrast to the Roman Catholic notion of original sin, articulated by Augustine, Celtic thinkers from Pelagius and John Scotus to J. Philip Newell affirm the essential wholeness of humankind. While our turning away from

---

[26] I prefer the term "everlasting" to "eternal" now in order to highlight the experiential embracing of changeless by that which changes, the abstract by the concrete, the stationary by the evolving, in the human, planetary, and cosmic adventures.

God and our earthly companions hides our original wholeness, this wholeness and beauty is never fully lost. We are born in love and die in love, and continue our post-mortem journeys in love.

In an age in children were expendable and often killed if they were born with birth defects, Jesus defied the cultural norms of the Hellenistic world by placing little children on his lap and embracing them with the divine hug. A small boy brings five loaves and two fish to the Teacher and a multitude is fed. When young Jeremiah protests his youth, the Holy Adventure challenges him to become a leader:

> Do not say, "I am only a boy" for you shall
> go to all to whom I send you, and you shall
> speak whatever I command you. Do not be
> afraid of them for I am with you to deliver
> you. (Jeremiah 1:7-8)

A perplexed young girl becomes the bearer of God's Incarnation. In her weakness and simplicity, she discovers that with God all things are possible and that her flesh and blood can give birth to the healer and savior. Aged Abraham and Sarah set out on life-changing journey into the unknown and give birth to a child whose descendents will change the face of the earth. Faithful Anna and Simeon await the coming of the Messiah and are given a vision of God's Shalom. They are now able to die in peace and wholeness, knowing that God's realm of justice and shalom is coming to earth.

> Master, now you are dismissing your servant in peace,
> according to your word; for my eyes have seen your

> salvation, which you have prepared in the presence of
> all peoples, a light for the revelation to the Gentiles
> and for the glory of your people Israel. (Luke 2:30-31)

Each stage of life has a gift for the journey. Like the child Jesus, we are challenged to grow in wisdom and stature, discovering our own unique voice and gift to the Holy Adventure. In the circle of life, even death praises the Eternal, for beneath the pain of death, we discover our own "place of resurrection." We begin a new pilgrimage in new lands with the Holy Adventure as our guide, companion, and friend. Surely, our times and places are in God's hands.

PRAYERS FOR THE PILGRIMAGE

Exercise One -Awakening to your "thin places." All moments are theophanies, revelations of the Holy Adventure, for those who awaken to the divine presence. Each moment is a potential epiphany, a revealing and awakening to the Divine. Walt Whitman once noted that "all is miracle." Abraham Joshua Heschel challenged us to see life through the lens of "radical amazement." In Celtic spirituality, certain places were set apart as places of divine revelation. These particular "thin places" inspired seekers to experience holiness in every place.

Awakening to the thin places of each day is a matter of grace and surprise – holy synchronicity –as well as openness. We cultivate openness through a commitment to spiritual awareness. There is no one path toward spiritual awareness, nor does any particular path insure that we will experience an epiphany. Still, when we seek the Holy

Adventure though meditation, prayer, imagination, service, quiet awareness, and commitment to justice, the light shines in unique ways along our path.

One way to experience thin places in your pilgrimage is to commit yourself to holy seeing. Just as the sculptor Michelangelo saw angels in boulders, you can look for God's disguises in every encounter and environment.

Look deeply in the face your child, spouse, or a friend. Listen to their words. Hear her or his deepest self revealed beneath their words and actions. Look for the inner light, the inner Christ, beneath the surface. See the holiness ready to leap out from tantrums and moodiness as well as kind words and loving touches. Act and treat them as holy children of God, poised to give and receive God's blessing through your love for them.

In everyday situations or challenging events, open yourself to the Holy Presence. Ask yourself, where is God in this situation? Is there an angel in this boulder? Can I experience grace in the manure of my life?

You may also awaken to the thin places in all things by going to particular holy places. Each area has places that speak forth the divine. For Celts, ancient and modern, the Tor of Glastonbury, the fabled Isle of Avalon; the Isle of Iona; and Findhorn are transparent to the divine. In my own journey, I find chimney rocks and seashore walks to be thin places. Ring Lake, Wyoming; Ghost Ranch, New Mexico; Pacific Grove, Santa Cruz, and Big Sur, California; Canyon de Chelly and Sedona, Arizona, and the Cliff Walk in Newport, Rhode Island, along with Iona and Loch Ness speak to the depths of my soul. The lower chapels at the National Cathedral in Washington D.C. are womb-like places of the spirit. The labyrinths at the cathedral at Chartes, France; Ring Lake in Wyoming; and Naramata Conference Center in British Columbia awaken us to the divine light on our path.

Still, in order to find a thin place anywhere, you must open yourself to the divine transparency everywhere. As Jesus said: "Ask and it will be given to you; search, and you will find; knock, and the door will be opened for you." (Matthew 7:7) With our Celtic spiritual companions as well as the Native Americans, take time to see your life as a pilgrimage, a vision quest, in which God constantly addresses you in thoughts, words, events, synchronous encounters, and friendships.

Exercise Two -Imaging God as your companion. Christ is our *anam cara*, the lover of our soul. God is our intimate companion and creative lure. Spirit is our life-giving inspiration. But, again, we must be awake to the grace that fills each moment.

In this spiritual practice, simply be still and ask for God to be revealed in your life. After a few moments, imagine yourself on a holy adventure, a search for your own Holy Grail, your own place of resurrection. What image do you have of the journey? What tangible or intangible reality motivates your search?

See yourself walking the pilgrimage of life. What does your environment look like? Who are your companions on the journey? What special moments have inspired you? What challenges have confronted you?

Now, in the midst of the journey, you discover that you have a companion – the Holy Adventure walks beside you. What is the appearance of the Holy Adventure?

What words do you say to the Holy One? In what ways does the Holy One respond? What wisdom do you receive for your pilgrimage? How does your self change through its encounter with the Holy Adventure?

Give thanks to the Holy Adventure for its inspiration and constancy. Remember that this wisdom is yours in every situation. Divine Radiance enlightens your mind and guides your footsteps.

Exercise Three - Praying the day through. We can pray without ceasing by remembering that God encounters us in each moment and event of life. Look at the day ahead. What moments call you to prayer? What actions do you regularly do each day? With whom do you typically spend your day?

Make a commitment to practice holy awareness in the day ahead. Take time to pray for each of your daily companions – for your spouse as he or she leaves for work or meets you across the breakfast table; for children going off to school; for the computer as you start it; for those persons whose notes are on your e-mail; for your dinner companions; for your workplace colleagues; for siblings and parents. In praying without ceasing, our days become holy, adventurous, and fresh. God becomes a living word that speaks through every occasion.

Exercise Four - Nothing Will Separate You From the Love of God. The spiritual journey is empowered by affirmations.27 Affirmations transform our minds and our

---

27 For more on affirmations, see Bruce Epperly, *The Power of Affirmative Faith: A Spirituality of Personal Transformation* (St. Louis: Chalice Press, 2001) ; Bruce Epperly and Lewis Solomon, *Mending the*

ways of seeing ourselves and the universe. The words of Romans 8:38-39 contain some of the most power affirmations for the spiritual path.: "Nothing will separate you from the love of God."

In your quiet reflection, ponder your greatest fears and worst case scenarios. Consider that which you deem God-forsaken in your own actions and the actions of others. Take time to ponder an alternative vision of reality, in which your deepest fears are embraced by Holy Love. You may choose to place each fear in the context of one of the following affirmations or create your own affirmations of faith:

> *Failure* will not separate me from the love of God.
> *Fear* will not separate me from the love of God.
> *Abuse in childhood* will not separate me
>   from the love of God.
> *Financial reversals* will not separate me
>   from the love of God.
> *Illness and death* will not separate me from the love of God.
> *Painful memories* will not separate me from the love of God.
> *Unemployment* will not separate me from the love of God.
> _____ will not separate me
>   from the love of God.

Exercise Five - Finding God in your life today. What stage of life are you in today -young adult-hood, midlife, eldership?

Take time to review your life. Where have you most deeply experienced God in your life? What moments

---

World: Personal Hope for Ourselves and Our Planet; Holy Adventure: Forty One Days of Audacious Living! (Nashville: Upper Room, 2008).

were pivotal? In what moments did you choose to say "yes" to the Holy Adventure?

Now, consider your life today. What are your challenges and limitations? What are your gifts? Do you experience God calling you through the challenges and gifts of life? Where is God being embodied in your life today?

Looking toward the future, where do you see the Holy Adventure leading you? What challenges lie ahead? What are your greatest hopes? What are your greatest fears? What dreams lure you into new frontiers of the spirit? Imagine God as going forward with you into the future.

Conclude with thanksgiving for the wisdom that has guided you in the past, the love that supports you in the present, and the creativity that lures you toward the future.

CHAPTER FOUR

CENTERED RELATIONSHIPS

Grace of the love of skies be thine,
Grace of the love of stars be thine,
Grace of the love of moon be thine,
Grace of the love of sun be thine.[28]

God is a circle whose center is everywhere and whose circumference is nowhere." All things are centered and encircled by Divine Love. Our spiritual journey begins with the exploration of our unique center of experience. As the philosopher Whitehead notes, "religion is what a person does with her or his solitariness."[29] But, then we discover that our unique and solitary experience is also relational and social. We are children of the universe. The universe in its entirety gives birth to each moment of experience. Indeed, healthy interdependence is the heart of reality. In a universe of relationships, the interplay of giving and receiving is a metaphysical and personal fact.

The sixth century monastic Dorotheos of Gaza affirmed that God is the center of the universe whose love

---

[28] From the Camina Gadelica, III, 215. Quoted in J. Philip Newell, *The Book of Creation*, p. 52.

[29] Alfred North Whitehead, *Religion in the Making, p. 47.*

draws each person simultaneously toward Godself and her or his neighbor. As we come nearer to our neighbor, we draw nearer to God. Conversely, as we more authentically love God, we more fully love our creaturely companions. In the words of the Desert Father:

> Suppose we were to take a compass and insert the point and draw the outline of a circle. The center point is the same distance from any point on the circumference....Let us suppose that this circle is the world and that God is the center: the straight lines drawn from the circumference to the center are the lives of human beings....Let us assume for the sake of analogy that to move toward God, then, human beings move from the circumference along the various radii of the circle to the center. But at the same time, the closer they are to God, the closer they become to one another; and the closer they are to one another, the closer they become to God.[30]

Self and other, individual and global, are joined seamlessly in the dance of Divine Creativity. In the context of divine omnipresence, you are always at the center of the universe. You are always the joy of the Divine Spirit. God loves you uniquely and completely, and is working

---

[30] Quoted in Roberta Bondi, *To Pray and to Love* (Minneapolis: Fortress Press, 1991), 25.

intimately in your life to bring forth your unique gifts. But, all things are also at center of the universe and God's intimate care. Every face you see and each bird in flight is also the joy of the Divine Spirit. God loves each one uniquely and completely, working intimately to bring forth their unique gifts. God numbers the hairs on every head. God treasures each lily of the field and companions the migration of each monarch butterfly.

The Word and Wisdom that gives life and beauty to the universe is also the deepest reality of each thing. Divine wisdom leaps off the pages of scriptures and holy books. Wisdom also sings in the melodies of the birds, echoes in the hooves of bison, and reaches toward heaven in the branches of the Douglas Fir. As the Talmud proclaims, "over every blade of grass, an angel hovers, saying 'grow, grow, grow.'" As we discover God in our own personal center, we experience God in the personal centers of others. As we claim God's presence through acts of affirmation and love in other centers of experience, we discover God's centering presence within our own lives.

Despite the harsh realities of global climate change, environmental pollution, disease, and terrorist threats, the universe, at its depths, is ultimately enchanted and friendly. We are inspired to combat the evils of the world precisely because the ultimate horizon of our lives is trustworthy and supportive in our quest for a more beautiful world. In recognizing the pain and joy of others as our own deepest pain and joy, we commit ourselves to bringing beauty to the earth.

Celtic spirituality is green spirituality. As Jesus of Nazareth proclaimed, all things find nourishment and life from the Divine Vine. (John 15:1-5) Connected to this vine, we are fresh, lively, vibrant, and fruitful. Each branch is essential to the health of the whole and the well being of every other part.

Contemporary theologians and mystics describe the universe as the Divine Body, within which each one of us is a center of energy and life. Without the part, the whole would be incomplete, and without the whole, the parts would perish. Similar to the organic relationship of mind and body, God is uniquely, but universally, present in each of the parts. Though certain parts are more experientially complex and self-reflective than others, each one matters. All things are windows to God in their own unique way. Finding our own center awakens us the Divine Center in all things. Freed from the defensiveness of the finite self, we become "mahatmas," large-souled ones, whose Christ-like presence embraces beauty and growth wherever it bursts forth.

The world sings the praises of God. God sings within each babbling brook, howling wolf, and soothing voice. With the Psalmist, we proclaim that everything is God-breathed and God-loved.

> Praise the Lord!
> Praise the Lord from the heavens;
> Praise God in the heights!
> Praise God, all angels!
> Praise God, all the hosts!
> Praise God, sun and moon;
> Praise God, all you shining stars!
> Praise God, you highest heavens,
> And you waters above the heavens.
> Let them praise the name of the Lord,

> For God commanded and they were created.
> God established them forever and ever;
> God fixed their bounds, which cannot be passed.
> Praise the Lord from the earth,
> You sea monsters and all deeps,
> Fire and hail, snow and frost,
> Stormy wind fulfilling the Divine Command!
> Mountains and all hills,
> Fruit trees and all cedars!
> Wild animals and all cattle,
> Creeping things and flying birds!
> Kings of the earth and all peoples,
> Princes and all rulers of the earth!
> Young men and women alike,
> Old and young together! (Psalm 148:1-12)

And the Psalms end with the affirmation that, in spite of the reality of pain and abandonment, the universe reflects Divine abundance – "let everything that breathes praise the Lord." (Psalm 150:6)

The human adventure is part of a greater cosmic adventure. Though our reflection of the divine image is unique, all things reveal the divine imprint. As one Celtic teacher proclaims, "the whole creation is brimful of the Divine presence and there is no place where God is not."[31] All things are objects of love and reverence. With all of creation, humankind groans as it struggles to embody its true divine destiny. We are not "naked apes," operating entirely in terms of conditioning and stimulus-response. Nor is the non-human realm brute and insentient. Every face and each flower reveals divine wisdom. All things are

---

[31] Anthony Duncan, *Elements of Celtic Christianity* (London: Element Books, 1992), p. 10.

lured by Spirit, permeated by Spirit, and treasured by Spirit. To find your own center is to reverence every other center.

Within the Celtic vision, mysticism is embodied and embodiment is mystical. Nature and grace are one. Loving God inspires us to love creation as the sacrament of Holy Wisdom. God is present in the wild energy of nature as well as its gentle face. God's voice is murmurs in the babbling brook and roars in the rolling thunder.

To those whose senses have opened to God's green grace, God blesses us through all created things.

> Power of storm be thine,
> Power of moon be thine,
> Power of sun.
> Power of sea be thine,
> Power of land be thine,
> Power of heaven.[32]

Human and non-human aspiration is joined in prayer and radical wonder. Enthralled by God's wonder bursting forth from ourselves, we sing the song of creation. Awakened to the divine voices of nature, we learn the song of our selves.

> Thine be the might of river,
> Thine be the might of ocean...
> The might of victory on field,
> Thine be the might of fire...
> Thine be the might of element...

---

[32] Carmina Gadelica, III, 231. Quoted in J. Philip Newell, *The Book of Creation*, p, 22.

The might of the love on high.[33]

Johns Scotus proclaims the universality of God's presence in words of praise, "All things are from God and through God and in God and for God."[34]   His words echo the wonder of the Psalmist:

O Lord, how manifold are your works!
In wisdom, you have made them all;
The earth is full of your creatures.
(Psalm 104:24)

Practical and life-changing mysticism arises from the love of God's green earth. As I gazed from cabin window at the Ring Lake Ranch, my soul was nurtured by the words of scripture and Celtic spirit guides. I feel the same wholeness as I walked the pathways or gaze at Lake Naramata that bounds the Conference Centre in British Columbia as I prepare for a lecture or workshop[35] But, the soul food that nourishes my being is also found in an encounter with a moose on a morning walk, the calm surface of the lake, the osprey carrying fish to its chicks, and the horses grazing in the meadow. I also experienced a holy gracefulness as I worshiped Saturday nights with our dappled and diverse congregation or gather with politically-

---

[33]   Carmina Gadelica, III, 237 . Quoted in J. Philip Newell, *The Book of Creation,* , p. 23.

[34]   Deirdre Carabine, *Johns Scotus*, p. 50.

[35]   For more about Naramata Centre, a retreat center related to the United Church of Canada, see naramatacentre.net.

concerned persons of all faiths to reflect on issues of justice as these relate to immigration or sexual diversity. God is present in action as well as in the silence from which intimacy, creativity, and justice-seeking emerge. As I turn on my computer to work on a sermon, write a few pages of a manuscript, or design an adult education program on faith and politics, my heart resonates with the musings of a Celtic writer of the eighth or ninth century:

> The woodland thicket overtops me,
> The blackbird sings me a lay, praise I will not conceal:
> Above my lined little booklet
> The trilling of birds sings to me.
> The clear cuckoo sings to me, lovely discourse,
> In its grey cloak from the crest of the bushes;
> Truly – may the Lord protect me! –
> Well do I write under the forest wood.[36]

In bread and wine, in chirping bird and flowing stream, in baby's skin and lover's touch, the word is made flesh and dwells among us full of grace, truth, and beauty. Nature is bread and wine for us, and so is the friend who embraces us, the child who takes our hand and points at a fluttering butterfly, and the spouse who pilgrims beside us from youth to age.

THE MANY FACED GOD

Many of today's spiritual pilgrims often assert, "I don't experience God in church or temple, but I see God

---

[36] De Waal, *Every Earthly Blessing*, p. 63.

most fully in nature." The assumption that God is absent from the human world of clothes, factories, and artifacts is a tragic distortion of God's aim for the universe. The reality is exactly the opposite. All things, including human beings, are partners, co-creators, and reflections of divine creativity. Though humankind most clearly hides the divine image through self-centeredness, injustice, violence, ecological destruction, and oppression, humanity is also the part of "nature" that most directly nourishes us. We spring forth from our mother's wombs. We hold one another's hands in times of celebration and desolation. We learn language, art, and dance from parents, teachers, and friends. Deep touches deep through the divine eros of lovers, the blessing of a bruised knee, and the comfort at the graveside. Friends of the soul and mentors help us find our true voice and sing with gusto.

An ancient story notes that when the gods sought to hide the ultimate truth from humankind, they buried the truth deep in the human soul, presumably, the last place we would look for divinity! We often forget that we are the center of divine love and creativity. Sadly we also overlook the fact that the divine center dwells in every other human being. Disguised though it may be by pain, addiction, harmful decisions, or alienation, the one who stands before you is the image of God, the word made flesh in this concrete encounter.

Jesus of Nazareth, saw the face of God in the most unlikely places – in lepers who were "dead men walking," in women who were judged incapable of spiritual growth or intellectual curiosity, in prostitutes bearing the projection of male lust and hatred for women, in diseased persons whose illnesses were judged to be the result their sinful behavior, in foreigners who were denied access God's presence, and in children who were expendable and often abandoned. To the Soul Friend of all, each face mirrored divine wisdom and beauty. Even the most disfigured visage, wounded by the world's hated or personal evil, hid a pearl of great price.

We are the enchanted children of an adventurous parent who created us for partnership and love. Embodying the love that brings forth galaxies and infants, we heal one another. We become the answers to each other's deepest longings and most intimate prayers. As we let go of the small, frightened and protective self, we grow into partnership with the Self of the Universe, and learn to bless and heal with every encounter. Every encounter reminds us that we are always on holy ground.

> When the Son of Man comes in his glory, and all the angels with him, then he will sit on his throne of glory....All the nations will be gathered before Him....Then the king will say to those on his right hand, "Come you that are blessed by my Father, inherit the kingdom prepared for you from the foundation of the world; for I was hungry and you gave me food, I was thirsty and you gave me something to drink, I was a stranger, and you welcomed me, I was naked and you gave me clothing, I was sick and you took care of me, I was in prison and you visited me." Then the righteous will answer him, "When was it that we saw you?"....And the king will answer them, "Truly I tell you, just as you did it to one of the least of these who are members of my family, you did it unto me." (Matthew 25:31, 34-37a, 40)

Our lives make a difference to God. By our loving acts, we heal the planet, mend broken hearts, and create a world that brings forth strong and healthy children. Every act of love is a gift to God, adding beauty to God's experience of the world.

You may be the answer to someone's prayer. You may be the Good Samaritan to an enemy or stranger wounded on the roadside. You may be the one who soothes the wounded heart, and feeds the famished child. You may be the only face of God that your brother or sister may see.

We are God's partners in the pilgrimage of Shalom. God's aim is toward wholeness, beauty, and abundance for all creation and each person. Our center blossoms as we nurture others. Our soul expands and unites with the Divine Center as we love the stranger and the enemy. This is a matter of both vision and action. When we are attuned to the Holy One, we see God in every face and share God in every act.

In his poem, "Call Me By My True Name," Vietnamese Buddhist monk Thich Nhat Hahn reminds us of the creative interdependence of all things that is the heart of compassion whether in the path of Gautama or the way of Jesus. Each center of experience uniquely encompasses every other center of experience. Each center of experience embraces the fullness of life from its own perspective. There are no distant and alien "others," only companions in the Adventure of the Universe.

> Do not say that I'll depart tomorrow
> because even today I still arrive.
> Look deeply, I arrive in every second

to be a bud on a spring branch,
to be a tiny bird, with wings still fragile,
learning to sing in my new nest,
to be a caterpillar in the heart of a flower,
to be a jewel hiding itself in a stone.
I still arrive in order to laugh and to cry,
in order to fear and to hope.
I am the mayfly metamorphosing on the
surface of the water,
and I am the bird which, when spring comes,
arrives in time to eat the mayfly.
I am the frog swimming happily in the clear
water of a pond,
and I am the grass-snake who, approaching
in silence, feeds itself on the frog.
I am the child in Uganda, all skin and bones,
my legs as thin as bamboo sticks,
and I am the arms merchant, selling deadly
weapons to Uganda.
I am the twelve-year-old girl, refugee
on a small boat,
who throws herself in the ocean after being
raped by a sea pirate,
and I am the pirate, my heart yet not capable
of seeing and loving.
I am a member of the Politburo, with plenty
of power in my hands,
and I am the man who has to pay his "debt
of blood" to my people,
dying slowly in a forced labor camp.
My joy is like spring, so warm it makes
flowers bloom in all walks of life.
My pain is like a river of tears, so full it fills
all four oceans.
Please call me by my true names, so I can hear
all my cries and laughs at once,
so I can see that all my joy and pain are one.
Please call me by my true names, so I can wake

up and so the door of my heart can be left
open, the door of compassion.[37]

Our true names reflect the Divine Image that gives
life to all things. Joined in Christ, the barrier of self and
other is broken. In seeing Christ's tear stained face in the
face of creation, we discover that we, and all other things,
are simultaneously both the "least of these" and the "holy of
holies."   Shalom and justice are the ultimate destiny of
all. The celebration of life, the feast of healing, embraces
humankind, and spirals forth to include the birds of the air,
the fish of the sea, and the four footed ones of earth.

St. Brigid, who embodied the Divine Feminine in
Celtic spirituality, envisages our heavenly home – the
destiny of all creation - as a grand party with Christ as the
host.

> I should like a lake of finest ale
> For the king of kings.
> I should like a table of the choicest food
> For the family of heaven.
> Let the ale be made from the fruits of the earth
> And the food be forgiving love.
> I should welcome the poor to my feast,
> For they are God's children.
> I should welcome the sick to my feast,
> For they are God's joy.
> Let the poor sit with Jesus at the highest place.
> And the sick dance with the angels.
> God bless the poor,
> God bless the sick,

---

[37] Thich Naht Hanh, *Peace is Every Step* (New York: Bantam,
1991), p. 123-124.

And bless our human race.
God bless our food,
God bless our drink,
All homes, O God, embrace[38]

God seeks abundant life for all. God invites us to become channels of abundance for everyone we meet. As process theologian David Griffin states, "God wants us to enjoy. But, God wants all of us to enjoy."

Awakened the Divine Center, our own true Center, we experience all creatures as companions, siblings, parents, and children. All things reflect the wondrous variety of divine artistry. All things are eternal and holy. In listening to their cries and seeing their true faces, our true voice echoes and our true face is revealed.

GREEN RELATIONSHIPS

God visits us in every encounter. Christ comes to us as the guest of each meal. The Spirit caresses us with every loving touch. The love that is universal is also intimate and personal. Still, we discover the true nature of God in certain holy encounters and green relationships that reveal our true center and inspire the soul's journey. Their verdant spirit frees us to be ourselves without judgment or condition. The green growth of our relationships mirrors the divine nurture of seedlings into sprouts and flowers. While every encounter is holy, I wish to celebrate the green holiness of the *mentor*, the *anam cara* or soul friend, the

---

[38] de Weyer, *Celtic Fire*, p 20-21.

spouse or life partner, and the *spiritual parent*. These unique relationships are the soil from which the divine bursts forth within our lives and our relationships.

The Magic of Mentoring. All encounters are vocational. Every relationship is intended to further the divine calling to wholeness and beauty in ourselves and another. All of us long to be noticed. While knowledge can often objectify and intimidate, authentic knowledge joins soul to soul. The Psalmist delights in God's knowledge of the totality of his experience, "Search me, O God, and know my heart. Test me and know my thoughts." (Psalm 139:23) Such knowledge unchains the spirit because it seeks only to enable us to grow into our deepest selves.

A mentor is one who notices you, picks you out in the crowd, and feels a particular affinity toward your unique spirit. Mentoring is akin to midwifery. In its co-creativity, it nurtures the conditions that give birth to our unique vocation. Global in scope, mentoring can embrace teaching a craft, a sport, an intellectual practice, a profession, or a technical skill.

A woman from one of my congregations once spoke of the great gift of an older lady who arranged the flowers for church each Saturday. Because she did not drive, she asked this teenage girl to be her chauffeur to church and back. Along the way, they talked about flowers, growing up, and God. No doubt the older farm woman never saw herself as a mentor, but she shared her wisdom and listened to the dreams of her young friend. The older lady died many years ago, but her young friend carried on the tradition of bringing beauty to church each Sunday for over three decades.

A professor notices the unique insights of an undergraduate student. Over weekly meetings at the university coffee house, the professor listens to his student's dreams, explores new ideas with her, and invites the student to see herself as a wisdom-giver in training. Years later the student becomes a master teacher and a leader in her intellectual field. To his delight, she introduces her mentor/professor to new ways of looking at the world.

A spiritual healer initiates a woman in midlife to the arts of healing and wholeness. While expecting excellence in her friend's work and commitment to her spiritual life, the healer gently reveals to her apprentice her own healing gifts and supports step by step her own growth as a healing partner.

Nearly thirty years ago, two ministers saw a theologian and spiritual leader in an unkempt "hippie" college student. They invited him to participate in service projects, to teach a theology class in church, and lead a nursing home worship service. If they had not seen more in me than I saw in myself I would not be writing these words today.

Mentoring is a gentle process of loving affirmation. While all relationships involve the interplay of giving and receiving, mentoring ultimately exists for the well being of the one who is mentored. To be a mentor is to selflessly let go of any preconceived image of who the other will become as a result of your mentoring. Recognizing the vocational nature of all relationships, a healthy mentor midwifes the emerging divine birthings in the soul of another. The mentor nurtures both roots and wings in the one he or she is called to guide.

The defensive   mentor requires obedience and thrives on control. He desires a student in his image and craves affirmation from the other.   When the student explores her or his own path or sings a different tune, the small spirited mentor feels threatened.   Authentic mentoring involves the graceful affirmation of one spiritual center by another.   Good teaching fosters creativity and freedom not conformity or rote learning. While structures are important, they are the prelude to improvisation and creative transformation.   Even, God delights in surprises and smiles as we chart new paths in the holy adventure.

Healthy mentoring creates an environment of spiritual, relational, and vocational freedom.   The good mentor knows that each person's path twists and turns in its own unique fashion. Mistakes and failures on the path are not a call to criticism or blame, but affirmation of new possibilities and unexplored territories. In the company of the healthy mentor, your center expands, your voice vibrates, and your heart glows. Imaging the encircling God that he or she embodies, the healthy mentor thrives on freedom, novelty, and creativity, and rejoices when the student explores paths the teacher has never considered. Good mentoring transforms a relationship from teacher and student, adult and child, to the partnership of fellow adventurers with the Divine Companion. Good mentoring reflects the Divine Mentor who brings forth our gifts, nurturing freedom, creativity, and novelty.

The Adventure of Anam Cara. St. Brigid is reputed to have said that "a person without an *anam cara* is like body without a soul." The Celts believed that spiritual relationships awaken us to our fullest potential.

Originating from the image of "one who shares a cell," the Celtic vision of the anam cara evolved to become "one who shares a soul." Our *anam cara* is our soul friend, the person who shows us the mirror of God in our own lives.

In Plato's *Phaedrus*, Socrates suggests that each person has an eternal mirror. Children of the same god, to use Plato's language, or soul friends, mediate to one another the essential wholeness and beauty that joins their spirits. Whether the *anam cara* is of the same or other gender, they are your "other soul," the embodiment of your spiritual pilgrimage in the unique life of another. When you discover the one you know as *anam cara*, you have a sense that you are one and that you no longer have to explain yourself or apologize for who you are. You are known, loved, and accepted without condition. Though soul friends have their own unique voice, they share a common spiritual melody.

In the Celtic tradition, Christ was known as the perfect *anam cara*. Christ is the intimate companion, whose love enables us fully to love the self we are becoming. Christ mirrors our deepest yearnings and brings them to wholeness. In experiencing the Christ as *anam cara*, we discover our true destiny as fully human embodiments of the divine wisdom.

Our human *anam cara* is our own personal Christ-figure, and the nearest thing to divine revelation in everyday experience. In knowing and being known, the Divine Eros gives life to both friends. Passionate in its mirroring and support, *anam cara* is, in the spirit of Plato's *Phaedrus*, a friendship that enables us to grow wings and fly to the heavens. As the mirror of Christ, the human *anam cara* inspires and lures us toward adventures of creativity and self-awareness. The Christ in us grows wings and flies.

Passionate without possessiveness, *anam cara* frees us to be fully ourselves in a holy relationship, which serves as the catalyst for the healing and transformation of all our relationships. In its greenness, it restores our spirits and gives us new life.

Your *anam cara* may be your husband, wife, or friend of the same or other gender. Regardless of the social relationship, the vocation of *anam cara* is to promote beauty and love in the world. *Anam cara* has as it mission service to all creation and transformation both of ourselves and the planet. In seeing the Eternal Beauty in another, our eyes are opened to beauty in all things. From that personal vision of beauty, we are inspired to be seek shalom and wholeness in our relationships and corporate lives.

As a holy and green relationship, *anam cara* compels each soul friend to aim at the highest ethical and spiritual values. Holy friendships, such as *anam cara,* enhance our marriages, parenting, and creativity, when it is lived out as the meeting of divine centers whose fullest expression does not necessitate physical proximity or sexual union. It neither "toils nor spins," nor competes with other relationships, but heals everything it touches. *Anam cara* inspires the muse within us to create freely and with abandon, whether poetry, sermons, books, music, or tales told at bedtime. Whether or not *anam cara* is joined with marriage, its embodiment is chaste and holy. *Anam cara* as holy relatedness vows to bring out the beauty in the other and to nurture the wingspan of the beloved friend in her or his context. The Divine Eros incarnate in *anam cara* friendships creates an environment that nurtures spiritual and creative quantum leaps.

According to certain strands of early Christianity, Christ reveals himself uniquely to each person. There are as many revelations of Christ as there are persons. The *anam cara*, embodying the Christ we share with another, is the image of God whose eyes stare deeply into our own and show us our true self. In knowing and nurturing the soul of another, our own souls grow in stature and soar.[39]

Holy Unions and Green Marriages.[40] In the biblical tradition, the primordial uniting of man and woman in marriage is described by these words:

> This at last is bone of my bones and flesh of my flesh....and the man and the woman were naked and unashamed. (Genesis 2:23,25)

Like *anam cara*, marriage and other committed relationships are meant to be bring wholeness to our lives. In another of Plato's dialogues, the *Symposium*, Socrates tells the myth of the origins of marriage and sexuality. Once upon a time, humans were spherical creatures, possessing four arms and four legs. Yet, in their wholeness,

---

[39] For one vision of *anam cara,* see John O'Donohue, *Anam Cara* (New York: Harper Collins, 1997).

[40] *In this section, I include, for brevity, under the umbrella of the word "marriage," all holy committed relationships, whether within or beyond the context of traditional marriage, as vehicles for divine wholeness and creativity. The image of God's ever-present center affirms relational and marriage equality as a reflection of God's quest for beauty and wholeness.*

they sought to challenge the power of the gods. In reprisal, the gods split each sphere in half. As a result of this primordial split, humans spend their lifetime in search of their other half, the one who completes their spiritual, emotional, and physical journey. This other half may be their spouse, lover, best friend, or *anam cara*. Still, the search is for the one person whose spiritual, emotional, and experiential patterns bring wholeness to ourselves and all creation.

Marriage and committed relatedness are quests for wholeness. Sexuality embodies in the physical realm the spiritual quest for union and centeredness with the other and with God. Whether we speak of heterosexual or homosexual unions, the goal of committed relationships is to incarnate wholeness at every level of life – mind, body, spirit, and relationships.

Marriage begins with a vision – the awakening to the deep spirit of another as joined with your own – and grows through an evolving vision, which explores the meaning of unity and diversity, same and other, yin and yang. Words spoken at the marriage of Kate Gould and Bruce Epperly on January 13, 1979 capture the many-hued beauty which emerges when unity and diversity are affirmed.

> Glory be to God for dappled things –
>   For skies as couple-colored as a brindled cow;
>   For rose-moles all in stipple on trout that swim;
> Fresh-firecoal chestnut-falls; finches; wings;
>   Landscapes plotted and pieced – fold, fallow, and plow;
>   And all the trades, their gear and tackle and trim.
> All things counter, original, spare, strange;
>   Whatever is fickle, freckled (who knows how?)
>   With swift, slow; sweet, sour; adazzle, dim;
>   He fathers-forth whose beauty is past change:

Praise Him![41]

Our partner in life truly is our "holy other." While the Divine Eros lures us to embrace and merge, this same Holy Eros reminds us that even in union, separateness must be maintained. The other is always "more" than we can imagine. In that more, the iconoclastic nature of life is revealed. As passionately united as a couple may be, there is still a place of mysterious otherness. That otherness may be the source of conflict, but it is also the well spring of novelty, adventure, freshness, and passion. In the spirit of Martin Buber's vision of holy otherness, the other's reality is not always understandable, but it is embraceable. Even when we cannot understand the other's words, we can lovingly share their lives.

The goal of marriage is to see and release the "angels within the boulders" of life. In profound concreteness, we experience the jagged edges of ourselves and another. Yet, beneath the jagged edge, the holiness of the other is ready to spring forth. A marriage of the spirit, like intimacy of *anam cara*, grows wings and expands freedom. In our quest for a holy union, God is the protean partner whose intimacy speaks through the holiness of the other to our own soul and gives birth to soulful beauty.

At their best, marriage and other holy partnerships are green relationships. Flexible, growing, fruitful, they flourish in supporting the growth and freedom of the other. Marriage lets go, so the other can grow! Within the

---

[41] Gerard Manley Hopkins, "Pied Beauty"

boundaries of each relationship, a healthy marriage promotes as much freedom as possible. In a holy relationship, we give one another "green lights" for our personal as well as communal pilgrimages.

Traditionally, marriage and, I believe, other committed relationships been seen as sacraments, and indeed they can be! For marriage makes holy the concrete life of diapers and dishes, embraces and arguments, passion and personal space. Marriage is the word of creation made flesh in the ordinariness of life. In the creative weaving of two souls with one another, the mortal takes on immortality and ordinariness becomes the window to eternity.

Passionate Parenting. Among life's synchronicities, and perhaps the most amazing meaningful coincidence, is the conception of a child. Often surprising and unexpected, the many become one and are increased by one, in the joining of a couple. A unique expression of the holy, this microcosm begins its own holy adventure in companionship with God.

To the newborn, parents in all their imperfection and uncertainty are the primary images of the Divine. In her interactions with mother, the child discovers the "feel" of the universe. Is the shape of the universe friendly? Does the cosmos supply my basic needs? Is life trustworthy? Do I matter just as I am? Is my experience of the world – my unique giftedness – affirmed and treasured?

While God transcends every image we can articulate, the image of the Divine Parent has both inspired and frightened persons throughout the ages. The Passionate Parent reflects the great love of a human parent for her or his child. In the biblical tradition, God asks the prophet, "Can a mother ever forget her child?" Jesus compares God to the Father, whose love responds to our greatest needs and whose will guides us toward our deepest self. The Holy One, like a mother or father, passionately loves each of her children, treasuring the uniqueness of each one and inspiring the growth of each one toward her or his true destiny.

Yet, some parents and some visions of "god" are destructive and narcissistic. The God of some persons reflects and inspires the most dysfunctional human behaviors. This God narcissistically requires the child to be his or her own personal mirror. Conditional in its love, this God condemns the initiative and uniqueness of any child who chooses to set out upon its own path. Relationship is a matter of obedience and submission. Survival requires abandoning our spiritual center and adopting the center of another.

Passionate parenting in the image of the Divine Center takes another path. Uniqueness is prized, creativity is treasured, adventure is affirmed, and interdependence is nurtured. Within structures of safety and bonds of love, healthy parenting launches a child on her or his own holy adventure. Ironically, healthy parenting involves a process of letting go - and of moving to the sidelines of a child's life - which enables the child to spread her own wings even as she embodies the parents' unconditional love and vision of reality.

Think of the journey of parenting. At first, mother is the universe in miniature. Her womb is the microcosm from which all blessings flow. Her breasts and arms are the "thin place" that sustains body and soul. But, the maternal universe is generous and trustworthy – in sharing its body with the child and in sharing the child with the father or other significant parent figure.

Life is a journey toward centered pluralism, a growing stature in which many faces come to define the nature of reality. The holy/wholly otherness of the mother grounds the child in holy interdependence. The child is the center of the universe, but she is not the only center of the universe. In meeting other centers, she discovers boundaries but also the richness of life. In the interplay of "yes" and "no," she glimpses her own self as a unique center of experience living in relationship with other unique centers of experience.

There is always "more" than her little world. And the "more" is stable and trustworthy in a world of change. There is a reality beyond herself that exists when she closes her eyes, when the door is closed, when parents journey to their own sacred space.

Rolling, creeping, toddling, walking, running – these are the seasons of life. Adventures of motion and adventures of ideas define the journey from womb to tomb. The first day of school, in which both parent and child learn to let go. Creative adventuring weaves together unbounded imagination with concrete actuality. Growing up involves receiving a vision, a dream, something to give your heart to, and then the journey to the land of self-centering and decision-making.

Wordsworth once noted that "the child is the father

to the man." Children are often their parents' greatest teachers. The toddler's persistence in rising and falling over and over again before that first fledgling step challenges the parent to face her or his own obstacles with grace and determination. The frightened child reminds the parent of the courageous adult that lies within each of us. The vulnerable child enables the parent to let go of what she holds dear for a higher cause. In mirroring our child's unfettered imagination and playfulness, we recover our own protean selves as we push beyond our own self-imposed limitations. We can take on new lives and embark on new adventures. From the joyful child's center, laughter, creativity, and high play spiral forth.

Passionate parenting holds and releases, protects, and challenges, structures and frees. Through it all, the passionate parent echoes the voice of Divine Creation: "you are beautiful, you are unique, you are gifted, and you can do it."

Roots and wings, centers and circles, an eternal home and a call to new lands – this is the Holy Adventure moving within our finite adventures. As Herman Hesse's Siddhartha learns, even the most enlightened parents must let their children explore the universe in their own way. They are God's children, not merely our own, and we must let them go into the arms of God with all our fear and trembling.

In its first months, the child learns to trust the universe. But, as the years go by, the parent must also learn to trust the universe – the small universe embodied in the growing child and the encircling universe that calls the child to adventure. At some point, the parent must learn to trust the child with the parent's own life. For just as once upon a time the child's unbounded spontaneity awakened our own oft-repressed freedom, now as parents we must trust our children, in the circle of life, to become our "parents," to feed and clothe us when we no longer can feed ourselves, to hold us when we are afraid, to soothe our pain and fears, and to sing lullabies of love when we face that greatest adventure – the journey from the familiarity of this earth to the unfamiliar horizon that lies ahead for us.

Yet, through all the protean adventures of parenting, we are always joined. As far as your child may roam emotionally or geographically from her original home, parent and child are still joined by the Divine Center in which all centers have a home.

HEALING CIRCLES

The center is everywhere. All centers join in a deep interconnectedness. The Holy Adventure awakens us each day with the dream of healing circles, celebrating and blessing both individuality and community. In our own centered self-creation, we shape the growth of others. We arise and are shaped from the divine and creaturely creativity all around us. Beneath the surface, circles of love join all things. When the defensive, protective self gives way to the greater self, we discover that we are blessed, whenever we bless others. In giving, we receive. In sharing, we abound in possessions. In letting go of control, the security of the universe flows through us. In healing others, we find our own wholeness.

PRAYERS FOR THE PILGRIMAGE

Exercise One - Holy Walking. Many of us live in an entirely human-made world. Surrounded by highways and shopping malls, we seldom experience nature in its wildness. Constantly driving from place to place, we rarely walk for the pure joy of it. Bombarded by cable television, CD players and iPods, and the sounds of traffic, we are oblivious to the chirping of birds or the howl of the coyote. Yet, creation is constantly singing. Beneath the surface of life, there is a deeper spiritual harmony – the harmony of the spheres of whistling wind, rustling tree limbs, and flying birds.

Whether you live in the city, suburbs, or country, take time to find the nearest faraway place – that intimate place of quiet beauty. Gently walk in this peaceful atmosphere, letting your eyes roam without any particular agenda. Prayerfully observe the trees and bushes, the birds and animals. Simply "be still" and awaken your senses to ever-present Divine Beauty.

Exercise Two - The Universe in a Grain of Sand. To exist is to dwell in the Divine Center. All things reach beyond themselves into the Infinity from which they come and to which they eventually will return.

Wherever you live, there are opportunities to see life more deeply. The art of seeing involves both observation and intuition. One way to see the Infinity in daily life is to meditate upon what is all around you.

For example, you may choose a blade of grass. Gaze intently at this blade of grass, noting its color, shape, size, intricacy. What does it smell like? How does it feel in your hand? Experience its uniqueness.

If you have a pet, or companion animal, take time simply to experience your pet on its own terms. Observe how it moves, the intricacy of its body, its responses to the environment, its concerns and passions. Know your pet as a unique center of experience, grounded in the Divine Center, and sharing in the Divine Passion from its own unique perspective.

Exercise Three - Seeing God in the "Least of These." God addresses us in every encounter. Yet, some faces seem to hide the divine, while others mirror holiness. We often hide from "least of these" – the impoverished, hungry, out of work, mentally ill, sick, and dying. To see their true divinity and beauty would call us to action. To see only their otherness enables us to distance ourselves from them and deny their humanity.

Jim Wallis of Sojourners tells the story of a woman who volunteers at a soup kitchen in Washington D.C. She addresses each of the persons who come down the line with a hearty welcome and smile, despite their smell or appearance. When asked why she is so friendly to the "down and out," she replied, "Someday, Jesus is coming down the line, and I want to treat him real good."

Jesus comes to *us* in the least of these each moment of the day. Yet, the least of these also express the many-faceted Divine Center. Our own vision is impoverished, when we fail to see the holiness their lives manifest.

In this meditation, simply be still and let go of your agenda. In the quiet, ask God to give you a new vision and guide you to see one of God's children from a new perspective. In this quiet state, let the image of one person who is among "the least of these" emerge. Look at her or his face, clothing, and demeanor. Hear her or his voice. Listen to her or his heart.

Experience God's presence emerging from them. See God's presence in their behavior and appearance. Awaken to God's presence beneath the surface of life.

Conclude by thanking God for revealing the deeper center that had been hidden from you. (You may choose this exercise as a way of making connection whenever you project your fear or anger on another person; when you feel especially antagonistic toward a political leader of our own or another country; or when a co-worker or acquaintance "pushes all your buttons" of insecurity, defensiveness, self-doubt, or hatred.)

Exercise Four - An Adventure in Mentoring. Relax either sitting or lying down. Let your mind roam as you ponder the important persons in your life, besides your immediate family.

What persons have positively shaped your life? What gifts did they bring to your life? What characteristics did they bring forth in your life? As you visualize these persons, give thanks for their impact on your pilgrimage.

Continue your meditation by reflecting on what persons you touch in your life. With whom are you called to share your wisdom? What gift are you called to share with them? Visualize this person (these persons) in the light of God. Give thanks for the opportunity to share God's wisdom with them. Ask for divine guidance in sharing your gifts in a way that supports their personal pilgrimage.

Exercise Five - Seeing the Divine in your Life Partner or Child. Each person is a unique incarnation of the Divine. Yet, often familiarity hides their uniqueness. We see them in terms of our needs and priorities rather than their own experience. Thinking we know them fully, we forget that each person is a divine mystery, revealing and yet hiding the fullness of God.

This prayerful exercise calls us to deep awareness of the "holy other" in our midst. Beginning with the prayer to see the other in her divinity, begin to let go of your needs, agenda, projections, or habits of relationship.

Listen to her or his voice. Listen to the word beneath the words.

Look upon her or his face. See the uniqueness of her or his face.

Listen to her or his dreams, spoken and unspoken.

Awaken to her or his pain, the hidden suffering, the brokenness revealed in words, posture, and asides.

Celebrate her or his beauty – of voice, face, embodiment, touch.

Let go of judgment and simply let her or him be the child of God that is revealing itself in the moment and waiting to reveal in the future.

Bless the other as you ask the Divine within her or him to give you a blessing.

Exercise Six - Affirmative Relationships. Life is centered, yet life is broken. All things are words of God, yet the divine speech is often garbled. In the interplay of our own brokenness and the imperfections of others, we often focus on the negative. Our irritations then lead to negative comments and hurtful behavior.

This exercise in healing begins simply with deep awareness. Spend a day simply observing your thoughts, feelings, and words in relation to an intimate person without judgment. These questions can also remind you of your own self-talk and quality of self-affirmation or negation. What is the quality of your language? Are you accepting or judgmental? How much of the frustration is born of your own brokenness? How much arises from the behavior of the other?

In the days ahead continue to observe your experience and language. Take a moment, without judgment, to reflect on the words you say before speaking. Do these words come from the divine center or from your fear and defensiveness? Do these words truly speak to the other's center?

Commit yourself to seeing the holiness and beauty that lies beneath the surface as well as the beauty of the surface. Whether the other is your child, spouse, or partner, take time to see the other as a unique center of God's love, a "holy other." Let your language reflect your changing attitude toward the other. Notice the "angels within the boulders" of your own and another's life.

As you share your feelings imaginatively with the other, speak from your truth rather than an abstract position. Share your deeper "I" as you address their deeper "Thou."

Realistically honor and praise the other. Share words of affirmation. Touch with gentleness and care. Take time to truly listen the other into speech and becoming as you treasure her or his own unique expression of the Divine.

As you begin to move from negative to affirmative language, you may need a place to start. Speaking from your own center, you may choose phrases such as these when they realistically reflect the other's experience.

> I am thankful that you are my husband/wife/child/friend.
> I love you!
> I enjoy seeing you _____.
> That's a great picture. Tell me all about it.
> I am so happy that you are my husband/wife/child/friend.

Often we are so wrapped up in our needs and our unique drama that we fail to experience the deeper lives of those who are nearest to us. We need to let go of our own need to be the center of life and remember that the other is also a divine center.

One way to discover the center of another person and help her or him bring forth that holy center is simply to ask questions and then listen without judgment. The following questions may seem quite pedestrian, but consider what might emerge if you truly listened to the heart of your spouse, child, parent, or friend.

> How are you feeling today?
> What would you like to do today?

What gives you pleasure?
What do (would) you enjoy doing?
What's your favorite book, movie, television show?
If you could do anything you wanted today, what would it be?
What is your dream for your life?
What is your favorite meal?
When do you feel happiest?
How can I support your journey?
What can I do for you?
Where do you experience God or holiness?

One of the greatest "journeys without distance" is the adventure of getting to know another child of God. Listening, questioning, sharing, affirming, and accepting open the door to holy connectedness, rekindled love, and deeper appreciation. Our eyes open to the unique depths of another from their vantage point rather than our own. In that holy appreciation, the walls of separation crumble revealing a frontier of love and companionship.

CHAPTER FIVE

THE ENCIRCLING GOD

Ageless and calm
Deep mystery
Ever more deeply
Centered in me....
Ageless and calm
Deep mystery
Ever more deeply
Centered in thee.[42]

God is the ultimate subject of the spiritual journey. God is the deep spirit of all things. When we speak about ourselves, we are really speaking about our relationship with the Holy Adventure whose circle encompasses us from birth to death. As we center in God, we discover that God has always been centered in us. As Augustine says, "You have made us for Yourself, and our hearts are restless until we find our rest in You."

Our lives are a journey with God as our most intimate companion. Whether our journey takes place amid dirty laundry and meetings to attend or leads to unexpected

---

[42] Adapted from a chant learned at the Shalem Institute for Spiritual Formation, Washington D.C.

destinations, we are lured onward by a Holy Adventure for whom no journey or adventure is too large or too small.

The Celtic vision sees God in all things and all things in God. God is the breath of life, the blood that courses through our veins, the roaring sea, the brightness of the sun, and gentle rain. A Celtic creed attributed to St. Patrick proclaims that Holy One is the lover of creation as well as humankind, bodies as well as spirits.

> Our God, God of all persons,
> God of heaven and earth, seas and rivers,
> God of sun and moon, of all the stars,
> God of high mountains and lowly valleys,
> God of heaven, and in heaven, and under heaven.
> God has a dwelling in heaven and earth and sea
> And in all things that are in them.
> God inspires all things, God quickens all things,
> God is over all things, God supports all things.
> God makes the light of the sun to shine,
> God surrounds the moon and the stars,
> God has made wells in the arid earth,
> Placed dry lands in the sea.
> God has a Son co-eternal with Godself....
> And the Holy Spirit breathes in them;
> Not separate are the Father and Son and Holy Spirit.[43]

Celtic spirituality provides an imaginative vision of God for the twenty-first century. The distant sky god, wielding thunderbolts and punishing wayward children with cancer and AIDS is dead, and deserves to be! The

---

[43] Adapted from Esther de Waal, *Every Earthly Blessing*, 55-56.

supernatural God, who leaves the world to its own devices, until "he" chooses to intervene with a miracle or natural disaster is irrelevant to the world of holograms, non-local causation, and ecological wholeness. The God who scorns the earth in favor a heavenly reward cannot respond to our needs for a holistic spirituality that unites prayer and protest, justice and healing, natural beauty and heavenly adventure.

THE ADVENTUROUS GOD

Many contemporary Christians have adopted the awkward word, *panentheism* to describe the reality that Celtic spiritual guides and theologians intuited a thousand years ago. Although the Holy Adventure is more than any one of us can grasp, all things dwell within this dynamic Adventure and this Adventurous One dwells in all things. The philosopher Alfred Whitehead, whose process-relational vision of reality has been a quiet companion on this Celtic journey, proclaims that:

> Every event on its finer side introduces God into the world....
> The power by which God sustains the world is the power of the [Divine Itself] as an ideal...the world lives by the incarnation of God in itself.[44]

God is the inner eros, or loving energy, moving in

---

[44] Alfred North Whitehead, *Religion in the Making* (New York: Meridian, 1972) p. 149.

all things and in each thing. Welling up within each experience, God lures each moment toward the divine vision of beauty and wholeness.

God is also in the restlessness within our hearts that pushes us beyond our comfort zones to our own holy adventures. It was God who lured me from the familiarity of my desk and books to the surprising dislocation of the corral, and God who rode with Jake and me over hill and dale. God gives the dream of walking to the toddler and the vision of new adventures to the elder. God was incarnate in Jesus of Nazareth, and God is incarnate in your life today. The God of Calvary was present with my family during my son's cancer treatments and the God of Resurrection was present in the prayers of friends and family across the world, the compassion and technical expertise of nurses and physicians, the flowing energy of massage therapists and reiki practitioners, and times of healing meditation and visualization. This same God is with you in health and illness, unemployment and retirement, and conflict and reconciliation.

Christ is our closest companion through the darkness and the light. Christ is the *anam cara*, the friend of every soul, "the mirror who discloses to every soul its greatness."[45] The wonder of all things is rooted in the creativity of the One who gives birth to all things.

The Celtic bards would have affirmed the sentiment of the Gospel of Thomas, "cleave the wood and I am there." Jesus' panentheistic image of God's energetic love in terms

---

[45] Ibid., p. 148.

of a vine from whom our lives branch forth reminds us that all life and creativity flows from the divine fecundity. All dualisms – mind and body, heaven and earth, spirituality and secularity, male and female, faith and science, this world and the next – are overcome and embraced by the Moving Center that encompasses all things.

A sermon from the Celtic monk Columbanus reminds us all things dwell within Divine Love and Care.

> Yet of God's being who shall be able to speak? Of how God is everywhere present and invisible, or of how God fills heaven and earth and every creature, According to the saying, Do I not fill heaven and earth? saith the Lord, and elsewhere, The Spirit of God, according t round earth, and again, Heaven is my throne, but earth is a footstool for my feet.....Therefore God is everywhere, utterly vast, and everywhere nigh at hand, according to God's own witness; I am, God says, a God at hand and not a God afar off.[46]

"God is a circle whose center is everywhere." God is the love that parents forth each moment of experience. God is the companion who guides us through all of life's adventures and challenges. God's erotic love envisions the wonder of your being and listens for your unique melody. God delights when the song you sing or the path you take has a lilt, melody, or curve that even God had not previously envisaged. With the Scot runner Eric Liddell, whose life was celebrated in the film, *Chariots of Fire*, we look at our own lives in their giftedness and rejoice, "God

---

[46] Adapted from *Living Between Two Worlds*, p. 76.

made me fast, and when I run, I feel God's pleasure."

God is the life-giving creativity that pushes forward children, planets, and galaxies. God is the inner light that guides each traveler's path. God is the womb from whose labors creation emerges one moment at a time. As the philosopher Whitehead asserts, "God in the world is the perpetual vision of the road which leads to deeper realities."[47]

God's circumference is nowhere. God includes all things in the Divine Experience. Each thought, prayer, and act finds an eternal home in God's ever-evolving vision of reality. With God, all things are cherished and nothing is forgotten. God's love gives an eternal meaning to even the most ephemeral acts. Again, the philosopher Whitehead notes, God is "the tender care that nothing be lost....the tenderness that loses nothing that can be saved."[48]

All things are loved by God, and nothing that is loved will ever perish. In ways that we cannot imagine, our lives become part of God's Everlasting Adventure. While Alzheimer's disease may riddle the mind, God never forgets who we are. We may fail at the tasks that lie ahead. Our adventures may be cut short by death, cancer, earthquake, or a terrorist attack. The pain of life may threaten to undermine our own personal centeredness. Still, each struggle, act of reconciliation, and quest for

---

[47] Alfred North Whitehead, *Religion in the Making,* p. 151.

[48] Alfred North Whitehead, *Process and Reality: Corrected Edition* (New York: Free Press, 1978), p. 346.

beauty, is treasured by God and becomes the material by which the Divine Artist brings forth new creations. In the call and response of God and the world, the philosopher Whitehead suggests that:

> The love of God for the world is...the particular providence for particular occasions....What is done in the world is transformed into a reality in Heaven, and the reality in heaven passes back into the world. By reason of the reciprocal relation, the love in the world passes into the love in Heaven, and floods back into the world. In this sense, God is the great companion – the fellow sufferer who understands.[49]

Your life truly matters. God is a different God because you exist. Your becoming shapes the Divine Becoming. Your life contributes to God's abundant life. The Universe is incomplete without your gift and your voice. Even if the quest for planetary wholeness fails or our planet perishes with the sun's final conflagration, what we do lasts forever. Within the Divine Memory, nothing is lost. God responds to "the insistent craving that zest for existence be refreshed by the ever-present, unfading impact of our immediate actions, which perish and yet live evermore."[50]

The Celts affirmed the wonder of all being. But, they also knew the earth to a wild place with unexpected snares and dangers. Even within the original wholeness of

---

[49] Ibid., p. 351.

[50] Ibid., p. 351.

creation were wild places where temptation and terror lurked. Pockets of chaos balance the orderly transformations of the Divine Center. But, chaos has its own wisdom, and beauty and adventure require a shifting balance of order and chaos and tradition and novelty. Still, these wild places can be overwhelming. Wildness is exhilarating, but it can also crush the spirit and maim the flesh. Amid gale winds and crashing seas, we find comfort in the presence of the Holy *Anam cara*. In the words of one pilgrim,

> God to enfold me,
> God to surround me,
> God in my speaking,
> God in my thinking,
> God in my sleeping,
> God in my waking,
> God in my watching,
> God in my hoping.
> God in my life,
> God in my lips,
> God in my soul,
> God in my heart,
> God in my sufficing,
> God in my slumber,
> God in mine ever-living soul,
> God in mine eternity.[51]

God encompasses us whether or not we consciously draw a circle around ourselves. The encompassing circles awaken us to a reality we often neglect when we are pushed

---

[51] *The Celtic Vision*, p. 12.

to the extremities of endurance by depression, pain, grief, or trauma. God's circle truly surrounds us. In the darkest night, we will fear no evil, including our own fears, because in both death and life, God's circle will hold. In that strong and safe circle, our own center holds. The Holy *Anam cara* will never fail us, even when we are most unprotected and vulnerable.

> Christ with me sleeping,
> Christ with me waking,
> Christ with me watching,
> Every day and night,
> Each day and night.
> God with me protecting,
> The Lord with me directing,
> The Spirit with me strengthening,
> For ever and for evermore,
> Ever and evermore, Amen.[52]

God is the mighty fortress that sustains us, the dream that inspires us, the second wind that empowers us, the courage that faces our deepest fears, and the home that beckons every adventurer.

THE CIRCLE OF LIFE EVERLASTING

As I gazed out the chapel window at Ring Lake each morning a few summers ago, I feasted on shimmering waters and towering mountains. But, what often caught my eye was the ghost-like shape of a dead tree, one of many that

---

[52] *Ibid.,* p. 12.

dot the ranch. As I looked more closely, I discovered that this tree was not really dead. Its dead limbs gave hospitality to nesting birds. The dead trees remind us that life emerges from death and that even in our own dying, we can build a lively foundation for ourselves and our companions on the journey.

The cosmic adventure weaves together in every moment the realities of birthing and dying. Each moment is a "place of resurrection," in which we must die to the past in order to embrace the novelty of the present. The evolution of persons and planets requires a constant process of creation and destruction. Despite the metaphysical necessity of death and dying, our death, and the deaths of those we love, remains a mystery that unconsciously shapes every step of our journey.

Among the Celts, death could come from any direction. Life was often short and death quick and painful. Life's brevity could not be denied by ventilators, medical marvels, or cosmetic surgery. Today, the realities of terrorism, global climate change, war, Alzheimer's, and natural catastrophes also remind us that there is no safe place to hide.

Death is the ultimate pilgrimage and adventure into the unknown. We can no more chart the territory of the afterlife than we can fully describe the Divine. Still, we live by hope that our place of resurrection will be a catalyst to future adventures. Though death can strike at any moment, we yearn for an abiding center that will not collapse in the greatest strains of life.

Our visions of God and of death go hand in hand.

Many travelers assume that with our final breath, the Divine *Anam cara* withdraws from our lives completely. With death, they affirm that our fate is sealed – we are ushered through the Heavenly Gates or abandoned to hellfire and brimstone, or we simply cease to exist except as compost for the next generation. They assume that the Circle of Love is completed at our deaths and that somehow those who die alienated from God and God's institutions fall beyond the reach and intention of Divine Love. But, the Circle of Love has neither beginning nor end. Spiraling forth into Infinity, this Circle embraces whatever has come into existence. Nothing is lost. All things are transformed in God's everlasting life. God will be "all in all."

Humility is an essential virtue for those who attempt to chart the afterlife. The Celtic vision simply affirms that the God of life is also the God of death, and that God of death is also the God of resurrection and new life. No one can fully describe the nature of this pilgrimage into resurrection. My own belief is that, beyond the grave, each being continues its personal and cosmic journey in companionship with the Holy Adventure, whose care encompasses any possible universe or realm of being.

The Holy Adventure continues beyond our deaths. We grow in wisdom in stature as we encounter our friends and family from this lifetime in novel and transforming ways. What was left undone relationally is healed and completed as the prelude to further adventures in God's Eternity. Lured by the vision of our stature as God's beloved children, we heal and are healed, we forgive and we are forgiven, we love and are loved in everlasting life.

Along the way, we may share in Brigid's feast of mead and song, celebrating Divine Abundance from a wider perspective than this mortal realm. But, the circle is unbroken. Loved once, we are loved forever. Awakened to the Holy Adventure, our pilgrim path stretches into infinity with each new adventure. Wherever we go, God's all-embracing companionship will be enough for the journey. With the Celtic hymn, we affirm that all of life's edges are places of resurrection:

Be thou my Vision, O Lord of my heart;
Naught be all else to me, save that thou art.
Thou my best thought, by day or by night,
Waking or sleeping, thy presence my light.
Be thou my Wisdom, and thou my true Word;
I ever with thee and thou with me, Lord;
Thou my great Parent and I thy true child,
Thou in me dwelling and I with thee one.
High God of Heaven, my victory won,
May I reach heaven's joys, O bright heaven's Sun!
Heart of my own heart, whatever betide,
Still be my vision, O ruler of all.

Though fear and darkness assail us, our trust is in the one thing stands firm, we will dwell in the Divine Circle forever.

PRAYERS FOR THE PILGRIMAGE

We conclude our reflections on the Divine Circle simply by quietly placing the future in God's hands. Take time to read Romans 8, pondering Paul's affirmation that "nothing can separate us from the love of God." Visualize yourself surrounded by permeable, but protective, light. This light protects you wherever you go as it encompasses both space and time. As you reflect on this light, envisage it stretching forth in time. Imagine it encompassing the next day, month, year, decade, and your whole life time. Imagine the great unknown of the death. How do you feel as you ponder the reality of *your* aging and death?

Visualize that light encompassing your final breath and surrounding you as you take the next steps in your spiritual journey. Visualize all time and space encompassed by this Holy Light. Experience the reality that all things are treasured in God's loving care. Imagine yourself always in the companionship of God's Loving Spirit...forever. With the Spirit as your companion, what adventures lie ahead for you? Where will you "go" on your holy adventure? Who are your companions on this adventure with God?

Conclude this imaginative prayer with words of thanksgiving to the Holy Adventure that encircles you. Whatever lies ahead, God's love surrounds and guides you, for "God is a circle whose center is everywhere and whose circumference is nowhere." Amen.

www.ingramcontent.com/pod-product-compliance
Lightning Source LLC
Chambersburg PA
CBHW032103080426
42733CB00006B/396